DISNEY THEME PARKS AND AMERICA'S NATIONAL NARRATIVES

Disney Theme Parks and America's National Narratives takes a public history approach to situating the physical spaces of the Disney brand within memory and identity studies.

For over 65 years, Disney's theme parks have been important locations for the formation and negotiation of the collective memory of the American narrative. Disney's success as one of America's most prolific storytellers, its rise as a symbol of America itself, and its creation of theme parks that immerse visitors in three-dimensional versions of certain "American" values and historic myths have both echoed and shaped the way the American people see themselves. Like all versions of the American narrative, Disney's vision serves to reassure us, affirm our shared values, and unite a diverse group of people under a distinctly American identity—or at least, it did. The book shows how the status Disney obtained led the public to use them both as touchstones of identity and as spaces to influence the American identity writ large. This volume also examines the following:

- how Disney's original cartoons and live-action entertainment offerings drew from American folk history and ideals
- how their work during World War II cemented them as an American symbol at home and abroad
- how the materialization of the American themes already espoused by the brand at their theme parks created a place where collective memory lives
- how legitimization by presidents and other national figures gave the theme parks standing no other entertainment space has
- how Disney has changed alongside the American people and continues to do so today

This book will be of interest to students and scholars of history, media, cultural studies, American studies and tourism.

Bethanee Bemis is a museum specialist in the Division of Political and Military History at the National Museum of American History, Smithsonian Institution, where she most recently curated an exhibition on the Disney Parks, *"Mirror, Mirror: Reflections of America in Disney Parks"*.

DISNEY THEME PARKS AND AMERICA'S NATIONAL NARRATIVES

Mirror, Mirror, for Us All

Bethanee Bemis

Routledge
Taylor & Francis Group

NEW YORK AND LONDON

Cover image: Orlando, Florida. May 10, 2019. Top view of Main Street and Cinderella Castle in Magic Kingdom at Walt Disney World. *VIAVAL/ Alamy Stock Photo*

First published 2023
by Routledge
605 Third Avenue, New York, NY 10158

and by Routledge
4 Park Square, Milton Park, Abingdon, Oxon, OX14 4RN

Routledge is an imprint of the Taylor & Francis Group, an informa business

ISBN: 978-1-032-32451-7 (hbk)
ISBN: 978-1-032-29498-8 (pbk)
ISBN: 978-1-003-31509-4 (ebk)

DOI: 10.4324/9781003315094

Typeset in Bembo
by MPS Limited, Dehradun

To my parents, who taught me to enjoy Disney World and sites of public history, my children, who are learning to enjoy the same, and my husband, who enjoys neither but loves me anyway.

CONTENTS

FIGURES

PREFACE

I once served on a panel with another public historian of similar age to myself (born in the late 1980s). We identified ourselves as being "of the Disney generation." By this, we meant that we had never known a world in which the Disney brand wasn't a dominant force in our everyday lives. For myself, I was brought home from the hospital to a Disney-themed nursery, I made my first trip to Walt Disney World at the age of two, and my first theater experience was watching *The Little Mermaid*. My mother had fallen in love with Disney World in 1979, and it was from her that I learned to appreciate the imaginary worlds within the Disney berms.

It was also from her that I learned to love public history; years of road trips to historic sites and evenings watching documentaries eventually led to my career as a museum professional. It was in 2016 while working to install an exhibition at the Smithsonian's National Museum of American history, that a line of inquiry opened that would bring these two formative influences in my life together. The exhibition under construction was *American Democracy: A Great Leap of Faith*, dealing with questions of how the United States had gone about crafting a nation after it had secured independence from Great Britain. It contained a section that posed the question of whether the new nation needed a national identity, specifically, a national narrative, and if so, who got to participate in crafting it, and where it was learned. The immediate answer that came to my mind was "Disney World." I realized that much of what I'd come to understand, on a personal level, as "American identity" was filtered through a Disney lens. This set me on a multi-year research quest to better understand the relationship between American identity, American history, and Disney theme parks, which has culminated in this book and a companion exhibition at the Smithsonian's National Museum of American History, *Mirror, Mirror: Reflections of America in Disney Parks* on display from Spring 2023 to Spring 2024. A major point in that research quest was the publication of an article of similar title to this book, "Mirror, Mirror for Us All: Disney Theme Parks and the Collective Memory of the American National Narrative," which appeared in the February 2020 issue of *The Public Historian*. I am grateful to the University of California Press for allowing me to reprint much of that article here.

There are many additional people and places to whom I owe my thanks for their contributions to this project. Professionally, I owe a debt of gratitude to Harry Rubenstein and Lisa Kathleen Graddy, who took a chance on me out of grad school and have continued to support me for over fifteen years now. Without their believing in me and providing professional resources and guidance, I would not have the career I have today. Claire Jerry has proved an indefatigable editor, and I am thankful to her both for helping me refine my many, many ideas and for smoothing the rough edges of my writing. Sara Murphy often took on the burden of work tasks we generally share for me when I was deep in this project, giving me the invaluable gift of time. To my NMAH lunch crew and text chain colleagues Frank Blazich, Kathy Golden, Molly Horrocks, Jennifer Jones, Cassie Mancer, Dave Miller, Dave McOwen, Sarah Oakman, Jane Rogers, Christine Russo and Melodie Sweeney, I offer thanks for professional advice, deep friendships and the providing of funny gifs to soothe moments of panic.

The Disney history community has been incredibly welcoming and supportive of my research, and I owe special gratitude to Dave Mason and Mindy Johnson for pointing me to resources and sharing their own vast knowledge. The public history community, too, has been overwhelmingly supportive, and I thank my grad school advisor Denise Meringolo most of all for her continued support many years after her official obligations to me were complete.

Without the encouragement and support of my family, I would never have found my career and my passion. Many years after the fact I thank my parents for taking me on so many amazing cross-country camping trips to National Parks, historic sites, and of course, Disney World. These trips laid the foundation for my career, and I apologize now for all the times I complained during them. I'm thankful to my mother Barbara for accompanying me on many research trips in the last few years, and to my father, Scott, for faithfully listening to me work through ideas out loud at our weekly dinners. To my brother, Ben, I am grateful to have had the pleasure of your company in my life and on still more research trips. My children Owen and Everett have also proven amiable Disney travelers. Each of their births spurred me to reach for new career heights and achievements, so while they don't know it yet, they are deserving of my thanks. Finally, to my partner Benjamin I offer appreciation for continually believing in me and supporting my interests (even when he doesn't share them), for keeping the house and family running happily when research trips took me away, and for being the one in our house who can always be relied on to make the coffee.

It truly takes a village, and I am thankful to have an incredibly wonderful one.

INTRODUCTION

Mickey Mouse sailed into American consciousness on November 18, 1928, in the cartoon short "Steamboat Willie." *The Washington Post* later observed that with this film, "Overnight Mickey became not only an authorized representative of the American people and the American scene, but an incentive to the laughter of nations."[1] While Mickey's ability to induce laughter was (and still is) instantaneous, his status, and that of the brand he represents, as an "authorized representative of the American people" was not, in fact, an overnight occurrence. It took years for the Disney brand to build the kind of cultural capital that allows the brand to act as a representative of the American people and years more for them to become the influential player in the identity of America as they are today.[2] In building that cultural capital the company built not only a well-recognized American symbol of their brand but physical locations for the collective memories of the American people and the "scene" they represent.

One of the most important ways culture and tradition pass from generation to generation is through the telling of stories. This is true not only on a familial and local level, but also on a national scale. Stories about American history that emphasize and illustrate the characteristics that make Americans unique create a national narrative that serves to reassure citizens, generate and affirm shared values, and unite a diverse group of people under a distinctly American identity.[3] This American narrative is kept alive through its retelling in literature, art and music, through its teaching in classrooms, and through the experiencing of it at sites of public memory such as National Parks, the Smithsonian Institution … and the Disney theme parks.

Disney theme parks are some of the foremost places where the nation consumes its collective memory of the American Experience, where they see many of the stories and cultural myths that make up the American national narrative. After all, Disney is in the business of selling memories. Not just memories of family vacations, but memories of stories from American history. Margaret King refers to the Disney

DOI: 10.4324/9781003315094-1

theme parks as a "'national trust' of mainstream cultural values" as imparted through these folk histories.[4] It is important to note that those "mainstream" cultural values and the historical stories presenting them were, at least in the early decades, skewed heavily white, male and middle-to-upper class.[5] This has changed over time, however, as the American "mainstream" has changed. The embracing of this change is an important factor in the continued success and cultural relevancy of Disney's theme parks, and the change itself can and should be understood as indicative of the evolution of the national narrative not just as represented at the Disney Parks, but at large scale.

The Disney theme park vision of America emphasizes the nation as a place of rugged individualism, free enterprise, and the conquering of new frontiers. It is a version of America that, in the words of Steven Fjellman, "taps into people's nostalgic need for a false history—for the reasonably benign makings of a community of memory. Disney has not only told stories to help fill out those memories but has become a central part of shared U.S. experience."[6] In what has become a rite of passage for the American middle class, millions trek yearly to Walt Disney World in Florida and Disneyland in California where they physically experience carefully curated moments of American history. By being offered the same impression of the American experience, visitors who come from different places at different times nonetheless share a collective memory. As Disney provides similar individual memories to more and more people who visit this happily nostalgic kingdom of American myth, their effect on American collective memory grows. While the entire Disney canon has a great influence on Americans' understanding of their history and shared cultural vernacular, it is at Disneyland and Walt Disney World that the American collective memory finds a physical place to reside. Disney's art, films and songs that so often capture American imagination are both born from and become part of American folk history. They are then funneled into the physical locations where their imagery is replicated, amplifying the cultural meaning of those spaces. Richard Francaviglia describes Disney's theme parks as maps that guests may physically follow, but also by which they "collectively get their bearings on the landscape of [American] imagination."[7] As Disney's art has taken on symbolic meaning, it is by overlaying these symbols on the map of the Disney theme parks that we make use of that meaning on a national scale.

While scholars do not generally agree on whether Disney's role in narrative-making should be understood as "good" or "bad," the historiography of Disney suggests they do agree that understanding Disney (not just the theme parks emphasized here, but all aspects of the brand) is an important key to understanding the American people. Mike Wallace, for example, while vocal in his concern that Disney trivializes history and obfuscates hard truths, is nonetheless also staunchly in favor of understanding the Disney theme parks as sites of public history. Henry Giroux, critical of a corporation having cultural power in a democratic society, still emphasizes that Disney does shape the national identity, even as he laments that they do so.[8]

Those who fall on the "good" or "neutral" side of the question frequently argue that any exposure to history is good for the public, whatever form it takes, or, as this book does, they attempt to understand Disney's cultural appeal in its historical context and relationship to its audience rather than seeing it as merely a corporation funneling ideals to the public.[9] Those who believe the Walt Disney Company's presentation of historical stories is "bad" most frequently cite concern over the type of history presented versus what is left out, and espouse fears over the implications of a corporation and its consumerist interests wielding cultural power for their own benefit.[10] These criticisms generally appear together, reflecting the assumption that a company whose livelihood is based on public consumption will present only certain aspects of history to remain popular, popularity giving them even more power to shape the views of history they propagate in ways that benefit themselves. While these criticisms are not necessarily incorrect and the connection between corporation and culture is certainly worthy of study, they are less than helpful for public historians or anyone attempting to understand Disney's role in public US-American life.

The Disney theme parks offer a useful barometer of the national narrative itself, at least in the way that many American consumers see it. What resonates with the theme park going public about Disney's representations of history? What do they push back on? Disney's presentations of the past at their theme parks have often been decried by those in the academy as a distortion of history, but this ignores the importance of what is actually occurring. What is occurring is not (and is not intended as) a straightforward history lesson one might get in the lecture hall. Instead, the parks provide a space to negotiate how Americans have understood and want to understand history. Most studies of the Disney Parks have focused on how Disney has packaged history for the public but have little acknowledged the way the public has influenced Disney's presentations. To gain a more complete understanding of how Disney grew to become an institution of public history, researchers must endeavor to acknowledge the *public's* role in doing so. We must meet the people where they are, and they are at Disney World.

Much of Disney scholarship until now has focused on singular aspects of the brand: cartoon and film critiques, art histories, business assessments, biographies of Walt Disney, and more recently, sociological studies of the theme parks.[11] While many pages have been written asserting the ideological importance of Disney theme parks in American culture, few seem to deeply question *how* that importance was achieved. How did the Disney theme parks become one of the chief purveyors of American history, and how do they maintain that cultural relevancy today? What is lacking from the current literature is an understanding of what built these spaces into what Robert B. Pettit called "shrines of the American civil religion" and why, when so many American shrines fall in and out of favor over time, they have endured as such for over sixty years. To answer those questions, we need to connect the various pockets of Disney scholarship into one narrative.[12]

The presence of so many distinct pockets of Disney scholarship can be in part explained by the fact that the term "Disney" can encompass many things. The Walt Disney Company as of this writing includes several production studios, media networks, five theme park resort areas, a publications arm, and more. This can make any discussion of "Disney" particularly difficult. In this book, when using the term "Disney" without qualifiers, I am referring to the brand at large and all it encompasses; the Walt Disney Company and its various holdings over the lifetime of the company. Though the book relies on every facet of the company to reach its conclusion, its focus is grounded in the theme parks, specifically those within the United States: Disneyland in California and the Walt Disney World Resort in Florida, with particular emphasis on Epcot and the Magic Kingdom. While those spaces are today the physical location of much of the negotiation and dissemination of the American national narrative, they became such in large part as an extension of the company's other endeavors in cartoon, film, music and television.

This book explores how five specific factors have worked in concert over time to transform Disney's theme parks from simple amusement parks to places where the collective memory of the American narrative is shaped: Disney's use of American folk tales and myths, the role of Disney characters as American symbols, the translation of folk history into physical experience, the legitimization of Disney's version of history through association with national figures and holidays, and Disney's continued use of and negotiation with history in their parks. Understanding these factors provides a framework from which to build toward a greater understanding of the ways Disney gained the cultural capital to become a recognized site of national collective memory. Such a framework will offer an avenue for both public historians and Disney visitors to frame their understanding of the Disney theme parks in a way that is useful for making sense of the Disney Park experience, as spaces where the American people negotiate the national narrative. While the first part of the book focuses on the how and why of Disney's rise as a disseminator and holder of the national narrative, the second part explores the role of the public in adapting the narrative at Disney to better fit the contemporary needs of collective identity-making within the United States. In so doing, it will show the Disney theme parks as not just bastions of a conservative, 1950s style "American Dream," but as places engaged with the public in the continual evolution of what it means to be "an American."

Notes

1 Quoted in Gary Apgar, *Mickey Mouse: Emblem of the American Spirit* (San Francisco: The Walt Disney Family Foundation Press, 2015), 101.
2 In this book, the term "American" is used to describe both citizens of the United States and those who claim identity as members of the United States population. While American is a term that could technically be applied to anyone in any of the countries considered part of the geographic Americas, since it is still, as of 2022, in general use as the term used for peoples of the United States, it will be employed in that sense here.
3 While acknowledging that there are many different narratives woven into the identity of those living in the United States, in this book the term "national narrative" is used to refer to the versions of American history, myths, and stories that are most commonly accepted and disseminated on official levels: in schools, at federal sites of memory, and by those wielding the most political and social power at any given time. This national

narrative is not fixed (an important factor in the conclusions of this book), so the use of the term isn't to denote specific stories or identities but rather to denote whatever stories are included in the national narrative at any specific point in time.

4 Margaret King, "The Disney Effect: Fifty Years After Theme Park Design," in *Disneyland and Culture: Essays on the Parks and Their Influence*, eds. Kathy Merlock Jackson and Mark I. West (Jefferson, NC: McFarland and Company, Inc., Publishers, 2011), 225.

5 This was reflective of the "official" national narrative as well, underscoring how Disney has been tied to popular ideas of American identity throughout its history: the first national historic site dedicated to a person of color wasn't officially dedicated until 1943, when the Disney company was twenty years old. In that year, George Washington Carver's boyhood home became a National Monument.

6 When Fjellman was writing two decades ago, his use of the term "false history" was meant to imply what I call "folk" history, that is, history taken from truth but massaged to fit a place and time. It does not refer to what today we might call "fake news" or "fake history," a phrase that has come to mean fact intentionally distorted for political gain. Stephen Fjellman, *Vinyl Leaves: Walt Disney World and America* (Boulder, CO: Westview Press, 1992), 60.

7 Richard Francaviglia, "Walt Disney's Frontierland as an Allegorical Map of the American West," *Western Historical Quarterly* 30, no. 2 (Summer, 1999): 166.

8 See Mike Wallace, *Mickey Mouse History and Other Essays on American Memory* (Philadelphia: Temple University Press, 1996) and Henry Giroux, *The Mouse That Roared: Disney and the End of Innocence* (Lanham, MD: Rowman & Littlefield Publishers, Inc., 2010).

9 See the work of Gary Apgar, Neal Gabler, Kathy Merlock Jackson, Margaret King, Karal Ann Marling and Stephen Watts.

10 See in particular Ariel Dorfman, Henry Giroux, Armand Mattelart, Richard Schickel and Mike Wallace.

11 When referring to Walt Disney, the man, I refer to him by his first or first and last name, as is done within the official literature of the company. Of course, separating the man from the company can be difficult in itself as Walt's reputation and own life story are as much a part of the Disney brand as Mickey Mouse.

12 Robert B. Pettit, "One Nation Under Walt: Disney Theme Parks as Shrines of American Civil Religion" (presentation, Annual Meeting of the Popular Culture Association, Atlanta, Georgia, 1986, revised 1992), https://www.academia.edu/1181176/One_Nation_Under_Walt_Disney_Theme_Parks_as_Shrines_of_the_American_Civil_Religion

References

Apgar, Gary. *Mickey Mouse: Emblem of the American Spirit*. San Francisco: The Walt Disney Family Foundation Press, 2015.

Fjellman, Stephen. *Vinyl Leaves: Walt Disney World and America*. Boulder, CO: Westview Press, 1992.

Francaviglia, Richard. "Walt Disney's Frontierland as an Allegorical Map of the American West." *Western Historical Quarterly*, Vol. 30, no. 2 (Summer 1999): 155–182.

Giroux, Henry. *The Mouse That Roared: Disney and the End of Innocence*. Lanham, MD: Rowman & Littlefield Publishers, Inc., 2010.

King, Margaret. "The Disney Effect: Fifty Years After Theme Park Design." In *Disneyland and Culture: Essays on the Parks and Their Influence*, edited by Kathy Merlock Jackson and Mark I. West, 223–226. Jefferson, NC: McFarland and Company, Inc., Publishers, 2011.

Pettit, Robert B. "One Nation Under Walt: Disney Theme Parks as Shrines of American Civil Religion." Presentation, Annual Meeting of the Popular Culture Association, Atlanta, Georgia, 1986, revised 1992. https://www.academia.edu/1181176/One_Nation_Under_Walt_Disney_Theme_Parks_as_Shrines_of_the_American_Civil_Religion

Schultz, John. "The Fabulous Presumption of Disney World: Magic Kingdom in the Wilderness." *The Georgia Review*, Vol. 42, no. 2 (Summer 1988): 275–312.

Wallace, Mike. *Mickey Mouse History and Other Essays on American Memory*. Philadelphia: Temple University Press, 1996.

SECTION I

Establishing Disney Parks as Sites of American Identity

1

DISNEY AND AMERICAN FOLKLORE: DISNEY TELLS AMERICAN HISTORY

Today The Walt Disney Company is recognized as a global empire with a diverse roster of products,[1] but in the very beginning (1923), there was only the Disney Brothers Cartoon Studio and their animated cartoons.[2] These cartoons often drew on American folk tales that had themselves evolved from historic myths and American ideals, telling stories that emphasized Americans' idealized versions of themselves. This wasn't particularly new; many films and cartoons drew and continue to draw on similar archetypes: the underdog turned hero, the pursuit of freedom, and humanity's relationship with nature, for instance. Historian Marshall Fishwick notes that "a nation's communal fears and ideals find their way into those media most immediately accessible to the people," which in the 1920s was often that offered at the local cinema.[3] What made Disney distinctive amongst the various cinematic offerings at that time was a combination of stunning artwork, innovative production techniques, and perhaps most importantly, a stable of re-curring and likable characters to star in these cartoons, led by the one and only Mickey Mouse. As these characters repeatedly starred in similar roles, audiences quickly discerned and began to identify with their representative personality traits, finding in Disney's entertainment both a reinforcement of the collective identity of the society they played to as well as lessons on what stories and individuals should inform that identity.

Mickey the Everyman

Out of all the characters today considered to make up the heart of Disney's cartoon canon (known by many as the "Fab Five": Mickey and Minnie Mouse, Donald and Daisy Duck, Goofy and Pluto) Mickey Mouse, in particular, emerged as a uniquely "American" character, cast in the roles of an average Everyman, of working-class Americans and of the folk heroes those Americans

DOI: 10.4324/9781003315094-3

looked up to. Even his origin story set him up as an American figure, with Walt Disney calling him a "symbol of independence."[4] While the exact inspiration for the mouse himself remains debatable, what is clear is that he was born from a moment of desperation on the part of the studio.[5] In 1928, the studio lost the rights to their original character, Oswald the Lucky Rabbit. More specifically, the studio discovered that they had never owned the rights to Oswald. It was a business lesson that would stick with Walt for the rest of his life. The character of Oswald had become popular, and the studio was looking forward to a bright, financially solvent future, until the distributor informed them that they were taking the character to be animated by a different studio who would produce them more cheaply than the Disney Studio did (and in perhaps an even more painful blow, they'd be doing it with many of the Disney Brothers' staff whom they'd hired away). The studio needed a new signature character, and Mickey Mouse was born.

Mickey, like the United States itself, was the result of a desire to escape from underneath a larger power who was treating the "underdog" or "little guy" in ways perceived as unfair. Walt leaned into this association, writing in 1948 (after Mickey had already reached incredible success), "Born of necessity, the little fellow literally freed us [Walt and brother Roy, partners in the studio enterprise] of immediate worry, provided the means for expanding our organization to the present dimensions and for extending the medium of cartoon animation toward new entertainment levels."[6] Even before his first commercial cartoon, before Walt and animator Ub Iwerks gave Mickey his "Everyman" personality, before American viewers laid claim to him as their native son, he was set up to shoulder the hopes and dreams of the Disney Brothers Cartoon Studio, not unlike when the newly formed American government was set up to shoulder the hopes and dreams of the nascent United States after its declaration of independence from Great Britain.

In the selection of the name Mickey, too, were similarities to choices made in the creation of America's founding identity. In setting up its government, America's founders chose to eschew many of the trappings of the monarchy they had left, opting (after much debate) for the banal "Mr. President" as the title for its chief executive, as opposed to the more flowery "His Excellency" or "His Highness." As art historian, Garry Apgar astutely observed, most cartoon stars of the 1920s, when Mickey was first drafted, had "oddly comical," almost aristocratic names such as Felix, Julius, or even Oswald. Following that tradition, Walt considered the name "Mortimer" for his mouse, until his wife, Lillian, told him it rang too "sissy" or "prissy." In choosing "Mickey" instead, Disney signaled that the character "would be much more his own man, and a more regular guy, as plain old 'Mickey'."[7]

A sampling of Mickey's early cartoons further illustrates just how strongly the Mouse was associated with American identity and folk history.[8] The first Mickey cartoon to be released, *Steamboat Willie*, drew heavily on a vision of an idyllic rural American heartland as well as the popular culture at the time, establishing its star from the outset as one who could identify with the American majority. *Steamboat*

Willie was a play on the popular film *Steamboat Bill, Jr.*, a Buster Keaton comedy that itself took inspiration from a familiar folk tune, "Steamboat Bill." In reflecting on Mickey's career 75 years after the short's debut, the Associated Press declared that in *Steamboat Willie* Mickey was established as "a symbol of American pluck."[9] Merriam-Webster's definition of pluck as "a courageous readiness to fight or continue against odds: dogged resolution" is a perfect definition for the side of themselves that American audiences saw and liked in their first taste of Mickey Mouse, the dogged resolution that was also echoed in both Mickey's and the United States' founding.[10]

In the 1929 short *Plane Crazy*, Mickey attempts (with mixed success) to fly a plane in order to emulate America's national hero of the day Charles Lindbergh, reflecting the dreams of many land-bound viewers following Lindbergh's famous solo flight across the Atlantic. Once again Mickey was pictured in the American heartland, a farm boy with big dreams and a whole lot of that "pluck" he had shown in *Steamboat Willie*. Again too, the short referenced contemporary American icons, this time via gags reminiscent of the silent film star Charlie Chaplin, a favorite of Walt Disney who later told a reporter that Mickey exhibited the "wistfulness" of Chaplin, a little fellow "trying to do the best he could."[11] Film historians note many of these "intertextual" references in several early Disney cartoons (Mickey's especially) that are drawn from and associate Mickey with popular stars of the day, including Keaton, Chaplin, and Douglas Fairbanks *(The Gallopin' Gaucho*, the second Mickey short to be released, parodied the Fairbanks film *The Gaucho*). As noted by Matthew Freeman these references branded Mickey "with the same outsider status that typified those screen comedians ... the working everyman quality ... an exemplar of everyman camaraderie."[12]

This outsider, everyman status was continually reinforced in Disney's films, resonating with audiences worldwide but especially in America. The foundational stories of the United States colonists as outsiders to the British who ruled them, and the myth advanced by Thomas Jefferson that America was an "everyman" nation of yeomen, not elite lawyers, had helped to craft into the national narrative the idea that American citizens together were outsiders and "everymen." In giving Mickey similar qualities, Disney colored him with a distinctly American identity. In 1933, Mickey was hailed by journalist Arthur Millier as

> an epic of your soul, my soul, the plumber's soul, and, of course, the soul of Walt Disney ... Mickey is 'Everyman,' battling for life and love ... He is honest, decent, a good sportsman ... Mickey has his little human weaknesses, but there is no question whose side he is on. He is little David who slays Goliath. He is that most popular, because most universally conceivable of hero-the little man who shuts his eyes and pastes the big bully in the jaw.[13]

Similar sentiments were echoed in media throughout the 1930s, such as this one in 1935 that claimed Mickey is not an animal; he is a personality, along with Uncle Sam, John Bull, Mr. Dooley and the Tammany Tiger. He is not a mouse at all; he is Mickey Mouse. In one way or another, since there is a bit of Mickey's helplessness, shrewdness, madness and mischief in the best of us, the nearest one in our day, to that mythical and ubiquitous fellow, Everyman.[14]

In short, Mickey represented the characteristics many Americans chose to see in their own histories and wanted to see in themselves, an archetypal American in all the best ways. Within a few short years, Mickey had gone from emulating American folk heroes to being one in his own right. "Like Uncle Sam or John Bull," wrote Marshall Fishwick, "the Mouse now has a separate existence off the drawing board. He belongs to those of us who accept him, as well as those who create him; he is public property ... a living graphic symbol."[15] Fishwick also noted "how much Mickey resemble[d]" Walt Disney himself physically, with "soulful eyes, pointed face, and gift of pantomime."[16] More significantly, many others identified Walt not with Mickey's physical form but with the uniquely American story he represented. Walt's own life story began in a midwestern farming town and eventually led him, through a series of business attempts, trials, and tribulations, to Hollywood success. Newspaper and magazine biographies of him in the 1930s often discussed Walt's humble roots to emphasize that his success came from hard work-as was, of course, the "American Way." The description offered by the *Daily Boston Globe* when Walt received an honorary degree from Harvard is typical of others at the time:

> *Snow White* has been seen by millions of theatregoers ... but the fairy tale that it presents is a mild, prosy children's bedtime story compared with the fairy tale of an uneducated but talented young cartoonist who used to swap cartoons with the town barber in Marceline, Mo., for haircuts, and now finds staid, old and moss-covered colleges, the upper realms of culture, competing for the chance to honor him.[17]

Walt's "fairy tale" rise from small-town boy to media mogul was positioned as "the old American success story of the self-made man overcoming obstacles on his way to fame and fortune."[18] The notion that Mickey's cartoons not only spoke to traditional American values but were themselves the products of one of America's own success stories gave them further credence as animated American representatives.

While the American public is always partial to an underdog story (or in this case, an under-mouse story), these themes were particularly popular at the time of their release because the United States was experiencing what would become known as the Great Depression. The nation needed not only a distraction from its troubles but affirmation that Americans had within them the qualities needed to weather the economic storm. Seeking comfort and reassurance, audiences packed theaters to see Disney's animated tales that offered what the *New York Times* columnist L. H. Robbins called "a nine-minute moratorium on the debt we owe

FIGURE 1.1 By the 1950s, Walt Disney had become such an American icon that he was frequently asked to pose for photographs when walking around Disneyland. Pictured here with Harue, Terri and Nancy Sumida

Source: Courtesy of Nancy Sumida.

to the iron facts of life" and the assurance of what Steven Watts termed "sentimental populism" to a country that sorely needed it.[19]

Buoyed by the success of the Mickey cartoons, popular both for their slapstick comedy and uplifting messages, Disney branched into other animated material, including the *Silly Symphony* series beginning in 1929 and the studio's first full-length film, *Snow White*, in 1937. The release of the *Silly Symphony* short *Three Little Pigs* in 1933 especially resonated with audiences. The moral of the story, a retelling of the fairy tale of similar name, is that hard work and preparation will allow one to triumph over adversity (just like Walt Disney). While the pigs faced a hungry wolf, Americans were facing an economic collapse. The film was so popular that it broke records in theaters, for both length of run and monetary gross.[20] This eight-minute, colorful reminder of persistence winning the day served, in the words of journalist Mayme Peak, "to restore America's old time cocky confidence." Peak referred to the short's song "Who's Afraid of the Big, Bad Wolf?" as "the new national anthem," noting

> We recognized in this and in them [the three pigs] something strangely reminiscent of ourselves and life ... Who's Afraid of the Big, Bad Wolf? Seven little words packed with the old-time optimism of America-herself-again![21]

The *New York Times'* John Black noted that the song "throws much light on American psychology," in that it encompassed the spirit of the United States not only during the Depression but in the face of all national crises, declaring that Americans could always "sing defiance loud enough and the wolf [would] depart."[22]

The short reinforced several aspects of traditional American character—the eventual triumph of hard work over all else, the willing defiance of the odds, and the victory of the little guy over a seemingly more powerful enemy. At a time of crisis, this reinforcement of collective identity traits helped to rally the nation to recovery. Professor Robert D. Feild wrote that "the lyrical jeer at the Big Bad Wolf contributed not a little to the raising of people's spirits and to their defiance of circumstance."[23] It also contributed to the association of Disney products with the collective American identity.

The studios' offerings of the 1920s through 1940s proved a balm for America's soul. As Walt Disney biographer Steven Watts summarized:

> For a mass audience of Americans suffering social and economic privation during the Depression, but yearning for a resurgence of hope, laughter, and faith in themselves, the social vision of Mickey Mouse, *Three Little Pigs*, and *Dumbo* proved to be both cathartic and reaffirming. In these films, as well as many others, Walt Disney wielded a political influence of which most politicians could only dream.[24]

That political influence was the kind that allowed Disney to both powerfully reflect and amplify the national narrative, as with Mickey Mouse, but also to help to continue to craft it. This crafting is well illustrated in the story of one of the Disney Studio's second-biggest stars: Davy Crockett.

Disney: King of the Folk Frontier

As the studio added live-action film to their repertoire of creative work in the late 1940s, they continued to produce stories drawn from American folklore, with films and TV series often explicitly recreating or fictionalizing historic events. Two combination live-action–animation films stand out in this regard: *Song of the*

South and *Melody Time. Song of the South* premiered in 1946, a film based in the antebellum south that used Joel Chandler Harris' Uncle Remus folk tales as its source material. Walt Disney chose the Remus tales because they had been, as he said, "in my mind from early boyhood," and because he saw them as an integral part of Americana:

> Their setting is in the romantic heartland of America: the fields and woods and dwellings of the pastoral South. Every youngster who has ever walked beyond the pavements, every American child who has ever read a school book, every grownup native of the land, is familiar with the animal counterparts of Brer Rabbit, Brer Fox, Brer Bear and their kin through which sagacious old Uncle Remus speaks the fabled wisdom of the ages … I take great personal as well as professional satisfaction in helping perpetuate for those who might in a hurly-burly generation miss them, the delightful stories of one of America's great writers.[25]

From Walt's words, we understand that part of his intention in making films based on American myths was explicitly to pass those myths down through the generations, a way of telling American children who they were. From the controversy that surrounded the film when it premiered, we get a glimpse of the way in which Disney as a brand became associated not just with the perpetuation of the American narrative, but also became a point of entry into and player in debates about what that narrative was and who should be included.

Song of the South was the first major Disney offering to elicit protest for the ways in which it depicted American stories and identity. The portrayal of Uncle Remus, formerly enslaved and now living as a freedman on the same plantation where his enslavement had been executed, "help[ed] to perpetuate a dangerously glorified picture of slavery. Making use of the beautiful Uncle Remus folklore, 'Song of the South' unfortunately gives the impression of an idyllic master-slave relationship which is a distortion of the facts," according to a statement by the NAACP at the time of the film's release.[26] Protests occurred at many of the theaters where the film was shown, with demonstrators often tying their protest directly to the fight black Americans were undertaking at the time for an equal place in society and the greater American narrative. Handbills distributed at a protest run by a chapter of the National Negro Congress at Broadway's Palace Theater in New York argued that the film was "an insult to the Negro people because it uses offensive dialect; it portrays the Negro as a low, inferior servant; it glorifies slavery and it damages the fight for equal representation."[27] This use of Disney-adjacent spaces and Disney-branded entertainment to debate the national narrative would increase over time, particularly after the opening of the Disney theme parks.

The second American folklore film released in this decade was *Melody Time* (1948), a compilation of both cartoon and live-action shorts that included stories of American folk heroes and featured current popular culture heroes. "The Legend of Johnny Appleseed" recounted the story of John Chapman, an American pioneer whose actual nursery-planting-and-missionary travels gave rise to a mythic life story that has come to emphasize his pacifism, rugged individualism, and conservation leadership as reflective of American values.[28] A second folk hero, this one entirely fictional, appears in "Pecos Bill," which told the tall tale of "the greatest cowboy who ever lived," who according to the legend created many of the natural landmarks in Texas with his bare hands. "Pecos Bill" was joined by several stars of the silver screen, including Roy Rogers and his horse Trigger. Rogers' constant portrayal of cowboys in Western film had created both he and his faithful horse companion as American folk heroes in their own right. Two of the shorts in *Melody Time*, "Little Toot" and "Trees" adapted American cultural offerings from other media: Hardy Gramatky's story of a New York City tugboat who learns a lesson about the value of work over play and Joyce Kilmer's poem about bucolic perfection. This collection, along with other Disney films of the same time period, spurred Hollywood critic Hedda Hopper to write that Disney's pictures were more and more "telling the stories of the all-American heroes of myth and legend, including Johnny Appleseed, Paul Bunyan, Ichabod Crane, Pecos Bill, Davy Crockett and others."[29] In the ensuing decades, live-action films became another focus of the Disney studios, still taking American stories as inspiration. *Johnny Tremain*, which told the story of a young silversmith in Boston, and the television series "The Swamp Fox," which featured the exploits of war hero Francis Marion, shared stories of the American Revolution. Films such as *So Dear to My Heart* and *Pollyanna* were adapted from American children's tales, while others such as *The Great Locomotive Chase* and *Ten Who Dared* were based on historical American figures.[30]

Perhaps the most famous of Disney's historic live-action films is 1955s *Davy Crockett, King of the Wild Frontier*.[31] Originally aired as three separate segments during Walt Disney's *Disneyland* television series, the stories proved so popular that Disney stitched them together and released them as one film.[32] The film touched off what became known as the "Crockett Craze," with merchandise so popular it was difficult for stores to keep on the shelves at times. While retelling a myth from America's collective consciousness, Disney also fostered new collective memories as the craze brought people together around their newly acquired television sets for communal viewing or gathered to discuss the latest installment. Outfitted in their official Crockett buckskin jackets and coonskin caps, children playacted the Crockett version of the American West, providing them a common cultural experience.

The lens through which Disney interpreted the mythic story of Crockett is representative of what became a hallmark of Disney's portrayal of the national narrative. Crockett was larger-than-life and somewhat idealized, but not so changed as to be unrecognizable to those who would know of him from studies of history. During the airing of the *Davy Crockett* TV series, one family wrote the Disney studio that if they didn't "get Davy out of the Alamo unharmed" they would no longer watch Disney's programming.[33] Disney stuck with the historically accurate, if less emotionally satisfying, ending, indicating that while they might be willing to play fast and loose with certain facts in the service of a good story, some historic moments were too important for even Disney to change.

This didn't mean, however, that the history they presented was entirely factual (nor did the company represent it as such). Disney's Crockett was "brave, intelligent, stalwart and kind," but Margaret King noted that this representation sparked public debate over whether or not it was accurate to the man himself.[34] Critics were answered by a passionate public that it didn't matter whether it was the exact truth or not-they preferred the model that Disney's Crockett offered to the children watching to one that was historically accurate. It is this ability to combine just enough historical truth with a hefty dose of idealization that gives the "Disney versions" such an impact. They are "real enough" that they take on the sense that they are "truer than true." That is, they tell versions of the facts that may not pass muster in a classroom, but perhaps more important, they tell a "truth" that many viewers want to hear and repeat to their children.

Today, Disney's Davy Crockett, and the many other historic characters the company interpreted, are implanted in our collective memory. This is due mostly to sheer popularity, the medium of television allowing it to enter the home and pervade daily life, and the appeal of Disney's stories reassuring narratives of American character during the post-World War II and Cold War era. The public was willing to accept some adaptations of fact in service of representing a character in ways that reflected traits they wanted their children to emulate. The more Disney's products played to the narrative of who and what Americans wanted to be, the more popular they became.

Where Mickey's cartoons had largely reflected American identity and values, the Crockett films and other accompanying history retellings moved Disney from a reflection of the national narrative to influencing what and whose stories were included in that narrative. Neal Gabler notes that in films such as *Davy Crockett*, "*Westward Ho the Wagons!* and *Johnny Tremain* "he [Walt] fashioned an American past of rugged heroes and bold accomplishment that for generations turned history into boyhood adventure" and in so doing "changed Americans' view of their history and values."[35] While stories of (largely white) Americans forging the Western frontiers had been integral in American identity since Frederick Jackson Turner first proposed his frontier thesis in 1893, Davy Crockett as an individual had largely faded from the pantheon of national heroes by the 1950s.[36] Margaret King notes that before the 1950s Daniel Boone was a more popular hero than Crockett in America, but he was supplanted in national imagination thanks to Disney's series and the fact that the "congenial, civic-minded Crockett" was more amenable to the culture of the 1950s than the "austere and antisocial" Boone. Disney's revival of Crockett's story brought him to popular thought so suddenly that the markets offering historical accounts of his life were ill-equipped to satiate the public's curiosity. Steven Watts reported that between 1954 and 1956 dozens of new historical accounts, including magazine articles, re-releases of Crockett's own autobiography, and a doctoral thesis from 1948, were rushed to print.[37]

Walt Disney himself noted his use of American myth in film and the role it played in the minds of viewers, describing the American identity as he saw it in these words, as reported by Hedda Hopper in 1948:

the heroes we made in our own likeness in this country are as good a reflection of our national traits and personality as anything history can offer ... Our pioneer forefathers created them-the Pecos Bills, the Bunyans, the exaggerations of a Johnny Appleseed from an actual wandering planter, the grotesque schoolmaster, Ichabod, the steel-driving man, John Henry, and a host of others-out of the needs of the times and the marrow of their bones. They were a household necessity along the expanding frontier ... In addition to the sheer entertainment values in the characters of our native legendry ... I think this is a good time to get acquainted with or renew acquaintance with the American breed of robust, cheerful, energetic and representative folk heroes. One thing they had in common-they were all workingmen. The mighty man of American myth earned his keep, riding herd, planting trees, felling timber, building railroads, pounding a steel drill, poling keelboats, taming nature in mighty joust and herculean feat. There were no drones in this great cast of national characters. They were just exaggerated portraits of the normal, busy, indomitable, toiling man of their day. And they are worth looking at—soberly and in fun—to re-educate our minds, and our children's minds, to the lusty, gutty new world called America.[38]

Disney's films were constantly reminding viewers, implicitly and explicitly, of the American character as Walt understood it. This was both part of what made them popular and what gave the films meaning to Americans beyond simple entertainment. They served as ways for Americans to pass on their values to their children and to understand their society. The films had become part of America's cultural artworks, to which the public looked for stories and symbols of their collective identity. Further, as with Davy Crockett and *Ten Who Dared's* hero John Wesley Powell, they held up individuals from American history as illustrative of who we should strive to be, reaching into the annals of history to select for viewers' attention those heroes whom Disney felt most worthy of venerating.

Disney's entire body work ultimately led President Eisenhower to call Walt Disney America's own "creator of folklore" in 1957.[39] Notably, Eisenhower repeated this point when he labeled Walt Disney an "Ambassador of Freedom for the United States" while awarding him the Freedoms Foundation's 1963 George Washington Honor Medal, the citation for which said Walt was to be honored for his "educational wisdom and patriotic dedication in advancing the concept of freedom under God" and "for masterful, creative leadership in communicating the hope and aspirations of our free society to the far corners of the planet."[40] It was this body of work—early cartoons as well as work on behalf of the government and American home front during the World War II—that initially created an association of the Disney brand and traditional visions of American morals and myths.

Notes

1 These include, but are not limited to, films, television shows, toys, games, music, books, magazines, theatrical shows and resorts. The scope of their product offering contributes to Disney's influence as it offers many avenues for individuals to come into contact with the company. Not all of Disney's products relate to American history and/ or identity; this book focuses on the significant number that do.

2 It should be noted that Walt Disney was involved in several other production companies before the Disney Brothers Cartoon Studio was opened, however, this is the date the present Disney company considers itself to have formally begun.

3 Fishwick, "Aesop."

4 Walt Disney, "What Mickey Means to Me," in *A Mickey Mouse Reader,* ed. Garry Apgar (Jackson, MS: University of Mississippi Press, 2014), 164.

5 The stories of where Walt's original ideas for Mickey were formed are varied: he was inspired by a mouse that sat on the desk in his early Kansas studio ... or was it his garage studio in California ... no, he didn't think about him until a train ride after a devastating business blow ... or maybe he was just Oswald, the first uniquely "Disney" character, morphed from a rabbit to a mouse ...—)

　　In recounting the possible tale of Mickey being dreamt up by Walt on a "west-bound" train on his way back to California from New York, news outlets will often unconsciously establish another association with the birth of American character-that it was forged in going "west." Garry Apgar attempts to untangle the many myths of Mickey's roots in *Mickey Mouse: Emblem of the American Spirit* (San Francisco: Walt Disney Family Foundation Press, 2015), 41–83.

6 Walt Disney, "What Mickey Means," 164.

7 Apgar, *Mickey Mouse*, 72.

8 These themes are of course not limited to Disney's Mickey Mouse cartoons. Art historians such as Garry Apgar and Steven Watts have documented the trend throughout the Disney brand's creative life as they expanded beyond their initial characters.

9 Mike Schneider, "Mickey Mouse, 75, represents U.S. culture," *The Times* [Munster, IN], November 18, 2003, A8.

10 *Merriam-Webster s.v.,* "pluck," accessed December 20, 2021, https://www.merriam-webster.com/dictionary/pluck.

11 Walt Disney quoted in Apgar, *Mickey Mouse*, 53.

12 Matthew Freeman, "A World of Disney: Building a Transmedia Storyworld for Mickey and his Friends," in *World Building: Transmedia, Fans, Industries*, ed. Marta Boni (Amsterdam University Press, 2017), 99–100.

13 Arthur Millier, "Disney's Artistry Explains Silly Symphony Popularity," *Los Angeles Times*, November 5, 1933.

14 Note the way the author likens Mickey to American folk personalities. L. H. Robbins, "Mickey Mouse Emerges as Economist," *New York Times*, March 10, 1935, SM8.

15 Fishwick, "Aesop."

16 Fishwick, "Aesop."

17 "Harvard Giving Disney Degree," *Daily Boston Globe*, June 9, 1938, 1.

18 Steven Watts, *The Magic Kingdom: Walt Disney and the American Way of Life* (Columbia, MO: University of Missouri Press, 1997), 42.

19 Robbins, "Mickey Mouse."

20 John Scott, "Three Little Pigs and Big, Bad Wolf Clean Up Millions," *Los Angeles Times*, October 8, 1933, A1 and Neal Gabler, *Walt Disney: The Triumph of the American Imagination*, (New York: Alfred A. Knopf, 2006), 183.

21 Mayme Ober Peake, "Who's Afraid of the Big Bad Wolf," *Daily Boston Globe,* October 29, 1933.

22 John Black, "Story of the Depression is Told in Song," *New York Times*, February 25, 1934.

23 Feild quoted in Gabler, *Walt Disney,* 186.

24 *Dumbo*, from 1941, features another main character (the elephant Dumbo) whose hard work and strength of character see him overcome obstacles placed in his way both by nature and human force. Watts, *The Magic Kingdom,* 100.

25 Walt Disney, "'Remus' Was a Challenge Walt Disney Discloses," *The Atlanta Constitution,* September 29, 1946, 4D.

26 Walter White quoted in Bosley Crowther, "'Song of the South,' Disney Film Combining Cartoons and Life, Opens at Palace," *New York Times,* November 28, 1946, 45.

27 The fight over the film would continue. It was re-released in theaters several times in the years since its premiere, the most recent being 1986, but has never been offered on home video in the United States. In 2020 Disney CEO Bob Iger stated that the film would never be released on streaming platforms, stating "I've felt, for as long as I've been CEO, that *Song of the South* – even with a disclaimer – was just not appropriate in today's world." A ride based on the film present at both Disneyland and Walt Disney World is discussed in Chapter 6. "'Song of the South' Picketed," *New York Times,* December 14, 1946, 18 and Tom Butler, "The film that will never be available on Disney+," *Yahoo!Money,* March 12, 2020, https://money.yahoo.com/disney-plus-song-of-the-south-bob-iger-122023864.html.

28 Howard Means, *Johnny Appleseed: The Man, the Myth, the American Story* (New York City: Simon & Schuster, 2012), 5.

29 Hedda Hopper, "Disney Brings Native American Folklore Characters to Public as Film Heroes," *Los Angeles Times,* May 9, 1948.

30 *So Dear to My Heart* was based on the book *Midnight and Jeremiah* by Sterling North, Pollyanna was based on the novel of the same name by Eleanor H. Porter, *The Great Locomotive Chase* featured the story of James J. Andrews, who commandeered a train to destroy Confederate supply lines during the Civil War, *Ten Who Dared* depicts John Wesley Powell, a Civil War veteran who led an expedition down the Colorado River.

31 Many historians and cultural critics have attempted to unpack this phenomenon. By far the most comprehensive treatment is Margaret J. King, "The Recycled Hero: Walt Disney's Davy Crockett" in *Davy Crockett: The Man, The Legend, The Legacy, 1786–1986,* ed. Michael A. Lofaro (Knoxville: University of Tennessee Press, 1985).

32 Disney embraced television early in its inception, while many other movie studios were wary of the medium. The first Walt Disney Productions television special aired in 1950, and the first Disney series, *Disneyland*, began in 1954. Bringing Disney characters into American homes familiarized even more of the population with the brand and greatly contributed to their success financially and as tellers of the national story.

33 "A Wonderful World," *Newsweek Magazine,* April 18, 1955.

34 Margaret King, "The Recycled Hero," 151–152.

35 Gabler, *Walt Disney,* xiii.

36 Disney's Westerns did not completely leave out characters of color or the differently abled, but they never gained the national prominence of Davy Crockett. It is telling that they did not become as popular as Crockett, though their stories often dealt with the same time period and themes, their races hadn't been as reflected in the popular conception of American national identity in the 1940s–1950s when they were released as they are today. *The Nine Lives of Elfego Baca* featured the "New Mexican Davy Crockett," the true historical figure of a 1880s sheriff today recognized as Latinx, the *Tales of Texas John Slaughter* featured a Black cowboy, 'Bat' or John Swayne, alongside 1880s Texas Ranger John Slaughter, and *Ten Who Dared's* hero, Civil War veteran John Wesley Powell, is missing an arm, as was the real-life Powell, whose right arm had been amputated. While the potentially problematic ways these characters were portrayed (Douglas Brode describes how in his initial appearance Bat has a "Tom-like tendency to refer to Slaughter as 'sir,' while John hails Bat as 'boy'") and by whom they were acted (Elfego Baca was played by Robert Loggia, a man of Italian descent), is beyond the scope of this writing, many others have written about them and Disney's treatment of race in film writ large, including Douglas Brode, Jason Sperb, Richard M. Breaux,

Eleanor Byrne, Martin McQuillan, J.B. Kaufman, Manisha Sharma, John Willis, and many more. Douglas Brode, *Multiculturalism and the Mouse: Race and Sex in Disney Entertainment* (Austin: University of Texas Press, 2006), 75.
37 Watts, *The Magic Kingdom*, 316 and King, "Recycled Hero," 142–143.
38 Hopper, "Disney Brings."
39 Thomas M. Pryor, "Disney is Saluted by the President," *New York Times,* February 19, 1957.
40 "Disney Wins George Washington Award," *Atlanta Daily World,* February 24, 1963.

References

"A Wonderful World." *Newsweek Magazine,* April 18, 1955.
Apgar, Garry. *Mickey Mouse: Emblem of the American Spirit.* San Francisco: Walt Disney Family Foundation Press, 2015.
Black, John. "Story of the Depression is Told in Song." *New York Times,* February 25, 1934.
Brode, Douglas. *Multiculturalism and the Mouse: Race and Sex in Disney Entertainment.* Austin: University of Texas Press, 2006.
Butler, Tom. "The film that will never be available on Disney+." *Yahoo!Money,* March 12, 2020, https://money.yahoo.com/disney-plus-song-of-the-south-bob-iger-122023864.html
Crowther, Bosley. "Song of the South,' Disney Film Combining Cartoons and Life, Opens at Palace." *New York Times,* November 28, 1946.
Disney, Walt. "Remus' Was a Challenge Walt Disney Discloses." *The Atlanta Constitution,* September 29, 1946.
"Disney Wins George Washington Award," *Atlanta Daily World,* February 24, 1963.
Disney, Walt. "What Mickey Means to Me." In *A Mickey Mouse Reader,* edited by Garry Apgar, 164–167. Jackson, MS: University of Mississippi Press, 2014.
Fishwick, Marshall. "Aesop in Hollywood: The Man and the Mouse." *The Saturday Review,* July 10, 1954.
Freeman, Matthew. "A World of Disney: Building a Transmedia Storyworld for Mickey and his Friends." In *World Building: Transmedia, Fans, Industries,* edited by Marta Boni, 93–108. Amsterdam, The Netherlands: Amsterdam University Press, 2017.
Gabler, Neal. *Walt Disney: The Triumph of the American Imagination.* New York: Alfred A. Knopf, 2006.
"Harvard Giving Disney Degree." *Daily Boston Globe,* June 9, 1938.
Hopper, Hedda. "Disney Brings Native American Folklore Characters to Public as Film Heroes." *Los Angeles Times,* May 9, 1948.
King, Margaret J. "The Recycled Hero: Walt Disney's Davy Crockett." In *Davy Crockett: The Man, The Legend, The Legacy, 1786–1986,* edited by Michael A. Lofaro. Knoxville: University of Tennessee Press, 1985.
Millier, Arthur. "Disney's Artistry Explains Silly Symphony Popularity." *Los Angeles Times,* November 5, 1933.
Means, Howard. *Johnny Appleseed: The Man, the Myth, the American Story.* New York City: Simon & Schuster, 2012.
Merriam-Webster s.v., "pluck." Accessed December 20, 2021. https://www.merriam-webster.com/dictionary/pluck
Peake, Mayme Ober. "Who's Afraid of the Big Bad Wolf." *Daily Boston Globe,* October 29, 1933.
Pryor, Thomas M. "Disney is Saluted by the President." *New York Times,* February 19, 1957.
Robbins, L. H. "Mickey Mouse Emerges as Economist." *New York Times,* March 10, 1935.

Schneider, Mike. "Mickey Mouse, 75, represents U.S. Culture" *The Times* [Munster, IN], November 18, 2003.

Scott, John. "Three Little Pigs and Big, Bad Wolf Clean Up Millions." *Los Angeles Times*, October 8, 1933.

"'Song of the South' Picketed," *New York Times*, December 14, 1946.

Watts, Steven. *The Magic Kingdom: Walt Disney and the American Way of Life*. Columbia, MO: University of Missouri Press, 1997.

2

DISNEY DIPLOMACY AND MORALE: DISNEY SYMBOLIZES AMERICA

As Disney characters and cartoons were reaching new heights of popularity at the end of the 1930s, World War II interrupted the studio's—and the world's—traditional operations. As they had during the Depression, Disney's cartoons continued to offer lighthearted entertainment to a public often hard pressed to find anything to laugh about. A Disney cartoon, *Mickey's Gala Premiere*, was the final transmission from the BBC television station in London before it went off the air on September 1, 1939, due to security concerns (it was feared that enemy planes would be able to lock onto the BBC's signal and use it as a target).[1] As screens went dark, it was a fitting message of defiance that the happy, ever hopeful Mickey Mouse was the one to sign off. While Disney's cartoons and comic strips had already been popular overseas since the time of their release, the work that Disney did for the federal government in service of the war effort would cement the company as a quasi-official American symbol, both at home and abroad, giving the Disney brand a role as an American ambassador that continues today.

Mickey Mouse Morale

From the very beginning of U.S. entry into World War II, the Disney Studio was at work on the home front. The day after the bombing of Pearl Harbor in 1941, U.S. Army troops charged with protecting the nearby Lockheed Martin plant in Burbank, California requisitioned half of Disney's nearby studio for their own use, literally turning Disney space into official government space. Soon, the rest of the studio was devoted to the cause as well, churning out military training films, government propaganda (provided at cost), and military insignia (which was provided free of charge). Disney's entire stable of characters, as well as their staff, were to be employed in the name of patriotism. Even after the troops had left the studio grounds, the work that was being done on behalf of the government required the institution of a strict

DOI: 10.4324/9781003315094-4

identification system for all employees and visitors, indicative of the studio's status as a "defense plant."[2] This represents the first time Disney-owned space was used expressly for purposes of influencing national identity, in this case by the government itself; later chapters will show this to be only the beginning of such a tradition.

One of Disney's most significant patriotic contributions was boosting morale for troops when they allowed and facilitated the use of their characters as insignia for all military service branches.[3] Company artists created images of Disney characters (as well as new characters or mascots done in the Disney style) for use by different military divisions, eventually providing insignia to almost 1,300 units in the U.S. armed forces. Requests were so numerous that, to even come close to keeping up with the demand, the studio had to set up a five-person team devoted to insignia under the lead of artist Hank Porter. When these military units went into service, both at home and abroad, they took a little piece of Disney with them, literally alongside the American flag, effectively lifting Disney's characters' status to symbols of America for all they encountered. Worn as patches on uniforms, printed on letterhead, or painted at large scale on the sides of airplanes and navy vessels, the insignia held personal meaning for users as both a connection to home and a reminder of the culture they were supposed to be fighting for. The characters were carried "much as a pilot or crewman might carry a religious medal to ward off harm," or as talismans of luck.[4]

The designs weren't just symbols for young GIs. They represented something to the rest of the world too: the Americans are here. Near the war's end an article about Hank Porter's Disney insignia crowed "when Tokyo is taken, Porter's creations will be along. If the Marines do it, they will wear his bristling devil-bull-dog on their

FIGURE 2.1 Don Ross (right) and a colleague pose with a patrol plane bearing the insignia of Civil Air Patrol Coastal Patrol Base No. 14, Panama City, FL, circa. 1943

Source: Courtesy of Donald Ross.

jackets; if the Army they will be emblazoned with any one of several hundred unit identifications."[5] Japanese politician Shintaro Ishihara remarked in 2005 that his famously anti-American politics "were formed during the war when he remembers being strafed 'for fun' by US planes 'with pictures of naked women and Mickey Mouse painted on the fuselage.'"[6] The image of GIs sporting Donald Duck and pals garnered negative or positive associations depending upon the ways they were encountered; in either case, they were very clearly identified as "American."

The insignia were prized symbols for civilians as well, appearing on a variety of publicly available items including collectible stamps and matchbooks. The collection of the insignia art by those at home was seen as a way for the public to connect with their fighting troops abroad and to take part in a patriotic duty that connected civilians to their nation in wartime. A selling point in one advertisement was that "the insignia on these stamps adorn the Bostons and the Liberators, the Airacobras and the Mustangs [fighter planes] that are fighting in Libya and the Solomons, in the Aleutians and over France" while another claimed they would "help you appreciate the heroism and activities of the United States Army and Navy air forces. They'll acquaint you with the deeply rooted traditions of each squadron."[7] An ad in the *Los Angeles Examiner* called the images "a realistic representation of the very life and soul of our gallant fighting forces" and by extension, the nation they represented.[8]

The embrace of Disney characters as mascots by those fighting in the 1940s was an outcome of the way the country had already integrated Disney characters and art as part of its identity since those characters took the entertainment stage less than 20 years earlier. As Walt Disney's daughter, Diane, who like many other American children collected the insignia designs in scrapbooks, told author Pete Martin, "Father had a feeling that most of our men in uniform had been raised on Mickey Mouse, and since they had helped make the Mouse a success by going to see him, the Disney studio owed them something."[9] So when the generation of kids who had grown up with Mickey as a defining icon of their own identity asked to have a bit of Disney to remind them of home, she added, "'How could you turn them down?' Father asks. They meant a lot to the men that were fighting."[10]

In addition to working with individual military units, Disney partnered with several government agencies to educate citizens and encourage them to do their part for the war effort. Effectively, the U.S. employed Disney to be part of its official storytelling and identity making at a time when the idea of a uniquely American identity was used as an important way to contrast the country with those it was fighting. Disney characters appeared on posters, in books, and even on war bonds to boost their appeal to children. Disney's animation techniques and characters were used for educational shorts, training films, and war-time-themed entertainment. For example, *The New Spirit* (1942) was meant to explain income tax laws enacted in 1942 to help fund the war.[11] *Donald Gets Drafted* (1942) provided entertainment aligned with current events and promoted patriotic service. *Der Fuehrer's Face* (1943) is one of the best-remembered examples of the ways in which Disney's wartime cartoon shorts were both home front affirmations of Disney's place in American identity and emissaries of American sentiment overseas. Donald is depicted dreaming he works in a Nazi munitions factory. Conditions are, predictably, awful and oppressive, and the short ends with Donald awakening in his bed and embracing the Statue of Liberty, crying out "Am I glad to be a citizen of the United States of America!" The title song (released in advance of the film itself) became immensely popular-the distributor became 350,000 orders behind on its record sales when it couldn't keep up with demand. One radio station auctioned off one of their few copies of the song for war bonds, and raised $60,000 worth in two days-fitting, since the theme of the short was that buying war bonds would help to sock it to Hitler-right in the face, as it were.[12] Journalist George Tucker remarked that the short and others of its genre represented "our national sense of humor reasserting itself." He also speculated that "if A. Hitler has not yet heard the Bronx cheer dedicated solely to him in the song called 'Der Fuehrer's Face,' he must be living a sheltered life."[13] Since the short was translated into most European languages and smuggled into occupied territories by underground resistance, he very well may have seen it, as did others outside the United States, a message of derision for fascism as well as American pride.[14] The Disney Company understood their role as American representatives in the shorts. Roy Disney wrote in an internal employee newsletter that the company's shorts "carry the message of America's might to all free countries."[15]

The Disney Company's involvement with the war effort established Disney as a truly American brand, pulling together with the nation in support of the American values their characters had already come to be associated with. Though other countries knew Disney characters as an American creation, during the war they were directly associated with the U.S. government. This was made explicit starting in 1941 when the Roosevelt Administration sent Walt on a tour of South America as part of the Good Neighbor program.[16] They hoped that Mickey and company (along with other human film stars) could inspire the countries of that continent to choose loyalty to the United States over joining forces with the Axis. Even if foreign citizens didn't find the American government all that likable, surely no one would want to stand against that lovable Mickey Mouse.

Walt Disney, the Best Neighbor

For the purposes of the U.S. government, the products Disney was to produce from the project were less important than the trips themselves. The programs put in place by Nelson Rockefeller as Coordinator of Inter-American Affairs to improve North and South American relations had, until the early 1940s, been at best unsuccessful and at worst damaging. While the idea of their relationship with Hollywood studios and artists was to integrate American and Latin American culture in artistic works that helped both cultures appreciate the other, the group went, in the words of J.B. Kaufman, "charging into their mission with far more enthusiasm than expertise ... their well-intentioned gestures frequently coming across as merely condescending or even insulting ... revealing their complete ignorance of Latin American political and cultural realities."[17] With Walt Disney, however, perhaps they could use an artist who *already* had fans worldwide, and capitalize on his popularity. The governmental authorization for the expenditure stated that "the objective of the project would be primarily to take advantage of Disney's goodwill and prestige which are unique the world over."[18] While the historical record isn't clear on whether the idea for a Disney South American tour grew from the government's directive for studios to produce more Latin American-centered content or was a direct ask from Rockefeller's office, it is clear that while there in 1941 Walt was used by the U.S. government as a cultural ambassador. He met with presidents, government officials and popular culture figures in every country, and his visit was covered by local media as well as back in the States. Everywhere he went the public came out in force to greet him. He was hailed as "a peaceful Ambassador of Humor" by Ramón Columba upon his arrival in Argentina and mobbed by fans in Brazil.[19] John Hay Whitney, reporting on Disney's initial weeks of travel to Rockefeller, wrote "Walt Disney is far more successful as an enterprise and as a person than we could have dreamed ... we had the right thought that he was the one representative we might send who above all others was outside the range of criticism."[20] Hollywood columnist Hedda Hopper anointed him "Good Neighbor Walt," and concluded "we couldn't send a better ambassador.[21]

The project resulted in numerous films and shorts that were released over several years. Today, the most well-remembered of these are the films *Saludos Amigos* and *The Three Caballeros*, starring Donald Duck, whom the *New York Times'* Theodore Strauss crowned an "ambassador-at-large, a salesman of the American Way" for his representation of the United States south of its borders.[22] These films, compilations of shorts that presented Latin American cultures filtered through a Disney lens, featured Donald Duck as, essentially, an American tourist-or ambassador-at-large, to echo Strauss. They were popular upon release in both the United States and Latin America. The media noted Disney's potential as a "hemisphere harmonizer," both with audiences in the U.S. to show them that they would "like very much these warmhearted people" to the south, and to South Americans. A Kansas newspaper suggested the United States' Southern neighbors had "taken Disney to their hearts and, by implication, the Norte Americanos. The picture may do as much as a dozen diplomats to seal friendly relations between the two continents."[23] Indeed, when a series of literacy and health films created at the behest of the Office of the Coordinator of Inter-American Affairs were screened in Ecuador, the undersecretary of education there referred to the project and staff as "effective missionaries of Americanism."[24]

At this point, the title "Salesman of the American Way," which Strauss had ascribed to Donald Duck, could really be said to belong to Walt Disney himself, as the use of his characters in war work had solidified his brand worldwide as a symbol of the United States and its values. After this, Disney and America would be irrevocably linked. In 1944, Hopper, after she had discussed with Walt Disney his contemporary projects and upcoming plans, alluded to this future:

The war's end may be a long way off but it's good to see that leaders are looking ahead and will be ready for the return of our boys who sacrificed their all to establish the rights of free men to live and raise families with the security we here in America have always known.

Walt Disney, who built a mouse into a household pet, is showing us the way.[25]

After the war, Disney characters continued to be treated as American ambassadors. Immediately post-war, the cartoon characters were "sent as ambassadors of goodwill to the liberated countries of Europe," though they were more accurately "returning" as many of the cartoons (along with other American-produced entertainment) had been banned under Nazi rule for what American media called their depictions of "freedom."[26] Military insignia featuring Disney characters continued to be created after the close of the war as well. Notably the 2,300th unique design was crafted in 1955, an eagle for the U.S. Air Defense Command, and more were done in the 1960s and 1970s for troops fighting in the Vietnam War.[27] Others originally created during World War II are still in use today, such as the angry Donald Duck who symbolizes the 309th Fighter Squadron of the U.S. Air Force. Disney art continues to be used in diplomatic relations as well.

In 1974 during a trip to Moscow by the Nixons, "Soviet and American press officials and some newsmen" were seen wearing small Mickey Mouse lapel pins.[28] The pins were being handed out by White House aide Tim Elbourne who was on leave from his job as vice president of Walt Disney Travel Company at the request of the Nixon administration. The gesture of humor and goodwill caused "mass doubletakes on the part of the foreign press corps," and provided a lighthearted moment of unity (as well as some good Disney PR).[29]

The first festival of Walt Disney animated films in Russia since the 1930s took place in 1988, with the first physical appearance of Mickey Mouse (as a costumed, walkaround character) in the Soviet Union's history being hailed as "a juvenile version of the Moscow superpower summit."[30] When Mickey met Russian Olympic mascot Misha the Bear, the security turnout was "worthy of a minor head of state," and indeed the moment was reported on as if the presidents of the two countries were meeting. Roy E. Disney, then-vice chairman of the Disney company, noted that "through the universal language of animation … we are taking one more step toward bringing our countries together."[31]

Even when not explicitly deployed by the United States as symbolic ambassadors, Disney characters are often understood as examples of successful "soft power" diplomacy. Because characters associated with Disney are representative of the United States, any time they appear globally, even as "knock-off," non-company sanctioned images, they are often read by cultural critics and politicians as representative of possible potential moments of softening toward American culture in countries often considered less than friendly to the U.S. North Korean leader Kim Jong-un is frequently noted in Western media for his enjoyment of Mickey Mouse and other Disney characters. A 2012 (unauthorized) appearance on

North Korean state-run media of costumed Disney characters dancing in front of an orchestra caused speculation the world over that it was a "coded message of new openness to the West," just as the acceptance of "iconic 'all-American' brands" in China had preceded official policy changes toward America there.[32] When CNN reported on one man's quest to visit all the world' s major theme parks in 2011, what they found most interesting wasn't his trip itself, but the "badly-copied Mickeys and Donald Ducks" he encountered all over the world. The outlet was particularly surprised by the presence of a smiling Mickey Mouse at the entrance to Eram Park in Tehran, Iran, where "Mickey Mouse, Donald Duck and the Seven Dwarves are not the U.S.-friendly images usually associated" with the country.[33] While a diplomatic visit from an American official might be out of the question for certain countries, the presence of Mickey and company offers "an effective channel towards further engagement' in places where "hard power means may fall short" in successful diplomatic relations.[34]

Disney Parks as Diplomatic Space

After Disneyland opened in 1955, it quickly became a popular space for cultural diplomacy, extending the symbolic use of Disney's works as American ambassadors to include Disney Parks. Often, Disneyland and (later) Walt Disney World have been used as official microcosms of America for visiting politicians and dignitaries; a way to show "America" to those only here for a short time-effectively holding up Disneyland as the most American of American spaces. In early years, the tours were often conducted by Walt Disney himself as the government continued to use him as an ambassador of U.S. goodwill.

Within five years of its opening, Disneyland had hosted Indonesian president Achmed Sukarno (1956), Prime Minister of Pakistan Huseyn Shaheed Suhrawardy (1957), King Mohammed V of Morocco (1957) and King Hussein of Jordan (1959).[35] King Mohammed would later tell an American journalist Disneyland was what he had enjoyed most about his United States visit.[36]

Both Disneyland and Disney World were looked to during the long, slow thawing of the Cold War as locations where Soviet ambassadors might get an overview of the best of America. In particular, the park was held up as both a place to gain an overview of American culture and an example of capitalism at work. One reporter wrote in a discussion of a potential visit by Soviet Premier Nikita Khruschev that "Disney could give Khruschev pointers on capitalism … The story of Disneyland is a tale of successful, clever, legitimate free enterprise in action."[37] While Khruschev was famously unable to visit during his 1959 U.S. tour due to security concerns, over the ensuing years Soviet delegations frequently toured both Disneyland and Walt Disney World, both from their own desire and at the suggestion of the United States, in efforts to experience America.

When plans were being formulated for a summit between President of the Soviet Union Mikhail Gorbachev and United States President Ronald Reagan, the idea of a Disneyland visit was floated numerous times as a way to show the General

Secretary of the Communist Party "American life typified."[38] It was reported that Reagan was hoping for a "'travelogue,' not a summit" where he could "show Gorbachev Disney World, escort him through a farm, introduce him to hot dogs."[39] In short, Reagan wanted to show Gorbachev symbols of "traditional" American life. Though Gorbachev himself didn't visit either park, choosing to remain in the District of Columbia for his visit, later Soviet delegates did. Viktor Nikonov, agriculture secretary, visited Epcot at Walt Disney World in 1987 with a delegation of 25 officials to better understand U.S. agricultural practices.[40] Col. Barney Oldfield, a press agent for Ronald Reagan during his time as an actor, was called upon by Reagan to, in his words "soften up" Mikhail Schkabardnya, Minister of Instrumentation, Automation and Control Systems. In a letter to Reagan, Oldfield, thrilled at how successful a tour he'd arranged at Disneyland had been, reported that Schkabardnya had told him that Gorbachev was interested in a Disneyland visit, suggesting that Reagan and his wife might want to "join them as 'tour guides for the day.'" "To heck with ping-pong diplomacy," Oldfield wrote, "how about in the Apollo-Soyuz space cooperative tradition, a little hand-holding of Mickey Mouse with the Matryoshka doll? It seems such a painless, but great, extraordinary international or foreign relations symbolism thing" to take the Minister—and Russian President—to Disneyland.[41] While Gorbachev never did make an official visit to Disneyland, the repeated suggestion that he should is indicative of the importance of the park as a representative American space.

It wasn't only Soviet government officials who were treated to a view of America-as-represented-by-Disney. Eleven-year-old Katerina Lycheva toured the United States on a goodwill tour in 1986, and Disneyland was her last stop. She was gifted "a symbol of all that is American-Mickey Mouse ears," though she didn't seem to understand the implications of having it on her head, reacting with a puzzled expression when a reporter asked if she felt "comfortable wearing a set of ears linked to the heart of American values."[42] A few years later a delegation of 90 Soviet sailors on another goodwill tour to the United States made Walt Disney World their first stop in a whirlwind four days. They were hoping to leave their trip "with an impression on how you live your life here" and at Disney World were "as impressed with American friendliness as they were with Mickey Mouse and Donald Duck."[43] Local papers reported that when the sailors rode Disney's Big Thunder Mountain side by side with American tourists, it was "a high point" of *glasnost*.[44]

Although he was ultimately unable to attend, President Richard Nixon had a speech draft prepared for his planned appearance at Walt Disney World's opening. The draft included a description of Disneyland as "a mecca for foreign tourists-including 11 kings and queens, 24 other heads of state, and 27 princes and princesses ... [Walt Disney] helped America speak to the world, and I know that tradition will be carried on here at Walt Disney World."[45] On that park's first anniversary, Robert Jackson, of the U.S. Travel Service, a division of the Department of Commerce, noted that "Walt Disney World has also played a very important role as a strong counter-balance to the negative sociological influences that have often injured the nation's image abroad."[46] Deputy chief of protocol for the City of Los Angeles Charlotte Asberry observed that by 1986 "it was easier to count those [dignitaries visiting Los Angeles] who did not go to Disneyland," than list those that did. Disneyland and Disney World have to this day worldwide reputations for being "clean and shiny and polite and happy and American" and they owe it in part to the reputations as such that Mickey and Walt established before their existence.[47]

The theme parks even came to be places used to represent America abroad when they couldn't be physically experienced. In 1975 a Russian television station ran a show titled "Magic of Disney World," which the State Department discussed in an internal memo sent from the U.S. embassy in Moscow to Washington, noting

> Deputy Foreign Editor Melor Sturua did highly positive voice over after introduction lauding Disney and Disneyland … such programming provides rare antidote to increased critical press play recently on hard times and social dislocation in U.S. Millions of Soviet citizens saw unusual glimpse of ordinary Americans not on unemployment lines or fighting busing in Boston, and Sochi will never look the same.[48]

Later the same year a visit by the Emperor and Empress of Japan was noted by the U.S. Embassy in Tokyo as having a positive impact on America's image abroad. Their "Disneyland visit [was] carried live on highly popular NHK "Studio 102" morning show, with camera switching between parade illustrating American history and shots of the royal couple in cozy group with American children." This, paired with coverage from the rest of the visit "provided Japanese viewing public with positive, multi-faced view of American society, culture and history."[49] Because "State Department officials have long known that most foreign visitors would rather see Disneyland than the Capitol or other soberminded American landmarks," the Art in Embassies program placed paintings of Disneyland on view in American embassies in Paris, Beijing, Moscow and Tokyo in the late 1980s.[50]

This image of Disney theme parks as examples of the "best" of America still resonated years later. In 1993 a visit from Princess Diana to Walt Disney World helped to rehabilitate British views of Florida, which had been suffering due to several crimes against British citizens that had recently occurred in Orlando. Diana reported the visit to be a "dream holiday."[51] After the terrorist attacks of 9/11 made tourists wary of airline travel, President George W. Bush used Walt Disney World as an example of places where the public should feel safe to go. "Get on board; do your business around the country; fly and enjoy America's great destination spots; get down to Disney World in Florida; take your families and enjoy life the way we want it to be enjoyed."[52] In 2012, President Barack Obama stood in front of Cinderella Castle at Walt Disney World to announce new ways to "pitch America as a travel destination for the rest of the world to come visit," declaring "America is open for business … Disney World and Florida are open for business … we want people all around the world to know."[53]

In their landmark study of how the Disney brand is understood and employed in identity-making worldwide, Janet Wasko, Mark Phillips and Eileen R. Meehan reported that, by the turn of the 21st century, almost 50% of global respondents indicated that they agreed with the statement that Disney was "uniquely American." Only 27.6% of respondents said it was not. This indicates that almost 23% of respondents fell somewhere in the middle, so that over 70% of those who answered the question felt that Disney was either definitely or somewhat "uniquely American."[54] Interestingly, the researchers found that the respondents' feelings on Disney and America were very much tied to one another. Whether they felt America was "good" or "bad," they transferred those feelings to Disney. This illustrated that "both of these camps ... seem to some extent to confound Disney and America: that is, anyone who was predisposed to like the U.S.A. can find support for this position in Disney representations. If, on the other hand, you view the U.S.A. as in some way disagreeable, then Disney can easily be seen as promoting everything you do not like about the country."[55] As with other symbols of America, the point of view one brings to the country as a whole is transferred to the symbol itself, in this case, Disney-branded products. This is true globally but is particularly strong in the United States, where citizens are quick to affirm or protest representations of the country through the Disney lens when products are introduced. Later chapters will explore what this means for the Disney theme parks, specifically.

Disney's war work and the subsequent use of Disney characters as American symbols went a long way towards giving the brand legitimacy as a representative of American identity, but it was not what made them unique in the formation of collective memory.[56] What truly set Disney apart from other American symbols was the creation of a physical place where the history and ideals they had become identified with came to life, so to speak, through lived experience. The use of Disney theme parks as representative American spaces flowed from the recognition of Disney the brand as an American symbol. An examination of those spaces and what they conveyed will illuminate why they were effective symbols of America's collective consciousness upon their creation—and how they retain that status today.

Notes

1 Finolo Rohrer, "Back After Break," *BBC News Magazine*, June 7, 2006, http://news. bbc.co.uk/2/hi/uk_news/magazine/5054802.stm.
2 See David Lesjack, *Service with Character: The Disney Studios & World War II*, Theme Park Press, 2014, 3–9.
3 Military insignia are signs or symbols used to mark ranks, functions, and units within the larger group. Specifically, the insignia referred to here were images used by individual units as a way to identify themselves. They often depicted Disney characters performing functions similar to those the unit might be tasked with. The design for Marine Scout Bombing Squadron 245, Marine Aircraft Group 23, for instance, shows Mickey Mouse astride a bomb while operating a machine gun with sights. While Disney did produce the occasional insignia for other Allied troops, the vast majority were for members of the United States Armed Forces.

4 Garry Apgar, *Mickey Mouse: Emblem of the American Spirit*, San Francisco: Walt Disney Family Foundation Press, 2015, 176; Frederick C. Othman, "Disney's Cartoon Factory All-Out For Buy A Bond, Pay a Tax Films," *The Miami Herald*, January 28, 1942, 9.
5 "Insignia Created by Busy Disney Artist," *San Fernando Valley Times* [San Fernando, CA], March 15, 1945, 1.
6 David McNeil, "Flags of Our Fathers: Commemorating Iwo Jima," *The Asia-Pacific Journal*, January 4, 2006, https://apjjf.org/-David-McNeill/2048/article.html. It should be noted, however, that the association between Disney and America for the Japanese had its roots in the 1920s and 1930s with the importation of Disney cartoons and merchandise being seen as representative of the United States, though this sentiment blossomed during and after World War II. See Shunya Yoshimi, "Japan: America in Japan/Japan in Disneyfication: The Disney Image and the Transformation of 'America' in Contemporary Japan," in *Dazzled by Disney? The Global Disney Audiences Project*, eds. Janet Wasko, Mark Phillips and Eileen R. Meehan (London: Leicester University Press, 2001), 160–181.
7 "Authentic, Official Airforce Insignia Stamps, Drawn by Walt Disney, to Be Distributed Free by the Press," *Pittsburgh Press*, October 14, 1942, 2 and "Albums Now for Combat Stamps," *San Francisco Examiner*, June 6, 1942, 7.
8 Quoted in Walton Rawls, *Disney Dons Dogtags: The Best of Disney Military Insignia from World War II* (New York: The Abbeville Publishing Group, 1992), 36.
9 Diane Disney Miller, *The Story of Walt Disney* (New York: Henry Holt and Company, 1956), 206.
10 Miller, *The Story*, 203.
11 Bob Thomas cites a Gallup poll suggesting that 37% of taxpayers reported a positive effect on their willingness to pay after viewing the short. *Walt Disney: An American Original* (New York: Disney Editions, 1994), 181–182.
12 George Tucker, "Manhattan The Matchbox Today," *Morning Herald* [Uniontown, PA], October 26, 1942, 4.
13 Tucker, "Manhattan." A "Bronx cheer" is a colloquialism for blowing raspberries in a derogatory manner.
14 Thomas, *Walt Disney*, 182.
15 Roy Disney in a 1943 issue of *Dispatch from Disney's*, quoted in Lesjack, *Service with Character*, 20.
16 The trips themselves and the products they produced have been well documented by other historians. See in particular J. B. Kaufman, *South of the Border with Disney: Walt Disney and the Good Neighbor Program, 1941–1948* (Glendale, CA: Disney Editions, 2009) and Theodore Thomas, *Walt and El Grupo* (Film, Theodore Thomas Productions, 2008).
17 Kaufman, *South of the Border*, 18.
18 Project Authorization, pg. 4, Nelson Rockefeller Papers, 1944–1955, Folder: Films, Walt Disney Productions, Rockefeller Archives Center, Sleepy Hollow, New York. https://dimes.rockarch.org/objects/Yirs6QfvnacZLbekSGjX4H/view.
19 Kaufman, *South of the Border*, 43.
20 Quoted in Kaufman, *South of the Border*, 37.
21 Hedda Hopper, "Good Neighbor Walt," *Washington Post*, August 29, 1944, 9.
22 Theodore Strauss, "Donald Duck's Disney," *New York Times*, February 7, 1943.
23 "Saludos, Amigos, New Disney Feat of Diplomacy," *Manhattan Mercury-Chronicle* [Mercury, Kansas], November 21, 1943, 5.
24 "Report on an Experiment of the Coordinator of Inter-American Affairs in the Use of Films for Teaching Health and Literacy," Nelson Rockefeller Papers, 1944–1955, Folder: Films, Walt Disney Productions, Rockefeller Archives Center, Sleepy Hollow, New York. https://dimes.rockarch.org/objects/Yirs6QfvnacZLbekSGjX4H/view, 39.
25 Hedda Hopper, "Disney Outlines Postwar Plans," *Los Angeles Times*, February 20, 1944.
26 Robert Myers, "Mickey Mouse Returns to War-Torn Countries," *Salt Lake Telegram*, May 25, 1945, 19.

27 Central Press Association, "Air Defense Command' s New Eagle 2,300th Disney Insignia for Military," *Morning Herald* [Hagerstown, MD], June 27, 1955, 4; "Disney Characters 'In Service' since WW 2," *Pittsburgh Post-Gazette,* January 3, 1970, 17.

28 United Press International, "Disney Aide Hustled Out of Kremlin Tea," *Los Angeles Times*, June 29, 1974, A11.

29 Associated Press, "Russia Certain of Detente," *Pensacola News* [Pensacola, FL], June 28, 1974, 2.

30 John-Thor Dahlburg, "Mickey Brings Disney Magic to Soviet Union," *Hazelton Standard-Speaker* [Hazelton, PA], Monday October 17, 1988, 13.

31 This display of unity was particularly meaningful given that Misha was the mascot of the 1980 Olympics, which the United States boycotted in protest of Russia's invasion of Afghanistan. Dahlburg, "Mickey brings."

32 Ed Hancox, "The Odd Disney Fetish of North Korea's Kim Family," *The Mantle*, accessed January 14, 2022, https://www.themantle.com/arts-and-culture/odd-disney-fetish-north-koreas-kim-family. Other media, however, also noted potential similarities between the "tight control" Disney exercises over their intellectual property and Kim Jong Un's desire to control his country. See John Feffer, "North Korea and Disneyland," *Institute for Policy Studies*, August 1, 2012, https://ips-dc.org/north_korea_and_disneyland/.

33 Barry Neild, "Mickey Mouse Brings Disney Diplomacy to Iran Theme Park," *CNN,* November 3, 2011, https://www.cnn.com/2011/11/03/world/meast/iran-roller-coasters/index.html.

34 Michael K. Park, "Long Shot: The Prospects and Limitations of Sports and Celebrity Athlete Diplomacy," *InMedia: The French Journal of Media Studies*, 6 (2017), https://doi.org/10.4000/inmedia.855.

35 Diplomat Julius W. Walker recalled that King Mohammed had enjoyed his official visit so much that he quickly returned incognito to experience it without ambassadorial fanfare. "We went back to town and the hotel about 4 o'clock. I found out later that Mohammed V changed his clothes immediately, put on a suit and went right back to Disneyland and stayed with Walt Disney until the place closed." Walker quoted in Liz Dee, "Disney World; The Happiest Meeting Diplomatic Place on Earth," *Association for Diplomatic Studies & Training,* July 11, 2014, https://adst.org/2014/07/the-happiest-diplomatic-meeting-place-on-earth/.

36 Drew Pearson, "Moroccan King Western Hope," *Altoona Tribune* [Altoona, PA], December 25, 1957, 4.

37 United Press International, "Will Nikita See Disneyland? No One Seems to Know," *Tucson Daily Citizen* [Tuscson, AZ], September 14, 1959, 38.

38 "Reagan/Gorbachev Summit Invitations Fall 1987," in James L. Hooley Files, Folder Gorbachev [Reagan-Gorbachev Summit, 1987] (7) Box 19290, Ronald Reagan Presidential Library, Simi Valley, California.

39 Mary McGrory, "New Summit Will Have to Be More Than Disney World," *Daily Item* [Port Chester, New York], July 22, 1986, 14.

40 Associated Press, "Soviets Visit Disney World," *AP News,* October 13, 1987, https://apnews.com/article/032364785cc468aeef3681c869b8fe61.

41 Letter, Col. Barney Oldfield to Ronald Reagan, James L. Hooley Files, Gorbachev [Reagan-Gorbachev Summit, 1987] Folder 8 of 11, Box OA 19290, Ronald Reagan Presidential Library, Simi Valley, California.

42 Bryce Horovitz and Victor Merina, "Disneyland Goes All Out for Katerina," *Los Angeles Times*, April 2, 1986, https://www.latimes.com/archives/la-xpm-1986-04-02-me-2376-story.html.

43 Amy L. Reynolds, "Soviet Sailors Make Revolutionary Disney Trip," *Orlando Sentinel*, July 18, 1991, 251.

44 Reynolds, "Soviet Sailors."

45 "Suggested Remarks for Walt Disney World," Richard Nixon Presidential Library and Museum, Yorba Linda, California, https://www.nixonlibrary.gov/sites/default/files/virtuallibrary/documents/jul11/gergen28.pdf.

46 Jim Korkis, *The Unofficial Walt Disney World 1971 Companion* (Theme Park Press, 2019), 282
47 Mrs. M. Hertzberg, "Sure It's Crowded, But It's Shiny, Polite, Happy," *Orlando Sentinel*, June 15, 1975, 36.
48 "TV Placement for IMV," Memo from the U.S. State Department, REF Moscow 18733, January 15, 1975, National Archives and Records Administration, https://aad. archives.gov/aad/createpdf?rid=122071&dt=2476&dl=1345.
49 "Weekly Highlights," Memo from the U.S. State Department, REF Tokyo 14458, October 1, 1975, National Archives and Records Administration, https://aad.archives. gov/aad/createpdf?rid=281367&dt=2476&dl=1345.
50 Sarah Booth Conroy, "For the Embassies: Disney Diplomacy," *Washington Post*, November 1, 1987, 145.
51 T. Barrientos, "Royal Residuals," *Philadelphia Inquirer*, August 28, 1993, 40.
52 George W. Bush, "Remarks to Airline Employees in Chicago, Illinois," September 27, 2011. Online by Gerhard Peters and John T. Wooley, *The American Presidency Project*, http://www.presidency.ucsb.edu/ws/?pid=65084.
53 Barack Obama, "Remarks at Walt Disney World Resort in Lake Buena Vista, Florida," January 19, 2012. Online by Gerhard Peters and John T. Wooley, *The American Presidency Project*, http://www.presidency.ucsb.edu/ws/?pid=97562.
54 Mark Phillips, "The Global Disney Audiences Project: Disney Across Cultures," in *Dazzled by Disney? The Global Disney Audiences Project*, eds. Janet Wasko, Mark Phillips and Eileen R. Meehan (London: Leicester University Press, 2001), 43.
55 Phillips, "The Global," 51.
56 Other studios such as Warner Brothers were also involved in war-themed entertainment work and employed by the federal government to sell bonds and moral lessons.

References

"Albums now for Combat Stamps." *San Francisco Examiner*, June 6, 1942.
Apgar, Garry. *Mickey Mouse: Emblem of the American Spirit*. San Francisco: Walt Disney Family Foundation Press, 2015.
Associated Press. "Russia Certain of Détente." *Pensacola News* [Pensacola, Fla.], June 28, 1974.
Associated Press. "Soviets Visit Disney World." *AP News*, October 13, 1987, https:// apnews.com/article/032364785cc468aeef3681c869b8fe61
"Authentic, Official Airforce Insignia Stamps, Drawn by Walt Disney, to Be Distributed Free by the Press." *Pittsburgh Press*, October 14, 1942.
Barrientos, T. "Royal Residuals." *Philadelphia Inquirer*, August 28, 1993.
Bush, George W. "Remarks to Airline Employees in Chicago, Illinois." September 27, 2011. Online by Gerhard Peters and John T. Wooley, *The American Presidency Project*, http://www.presidency.ucsb.edu/ws/?pid=65084
Central Press Association. "Air Defense Command's New Eagle 2,300th Disney Insignia for Military." *Morning Herald* [Hagerstown, MD], June 27, 1955.
Conroy, Sarah Booth. "For the Embassies: Disney Diplomacy." *Washington Post*, November 1, 1987.
Dahlburg, John-Thor. "Mickey brings Disney magic to Soviet Union." *Hazelton Standard-Speaker* [Hazelton, PA], Monday October 17, 1988.
Dee, Liz. "Disney World; The Happiest Meeting Diplomatic Place on Earth." *Association for Diplomatic Studies & Training*, July 11, 2014. https://adst.org/2014/07/the-happiest-diplomatic-meeting-place-on-earth/
"Disney Characters 'In Service' since WW 2." *Pittsburgh Post-Gazette*, January 3, 1970.
Feffer, John. "North Korea and Disneyland." *Institute for Policy Studies*, August 1, 2012. https://ips-dc.org/north_korea_and_disneyland/

Hancox, Ed. "The Odd Disney Fetish of North Korea's Kim Family." *The Mantle.* Accessed January 14, 2022. https://www.themantle.com/arts-and-culture/odd-disney-fetish-north-koreas-kim-family

Hertzberg, Mrs. M. "Sure It's Crowded, But It's Shiny, Polite, Happy," *Orlando Sentinel*, June 15, 1975.

Hopper, Hedda. "Disney Outlines Postwar Plans." *Los Angeles Times*, February 20, 1944.

Hopper, Hedda. "Good Neighbor Walt." *Washington Post*, August 29, 1944.

Horovitz, Bryce and Victor Merina. "Disneyland Goes All Out for Katerina." *Los Angeles Times*, April 2, 1986, https://www.latimes.com/archives/la-xpm-1986-04-02-me-2376-story.html

"Insignia Created by Busy Disney Artist." *San Fernando Valley Times* [San Fernando, CA], March 15, 1945.

James L. Hooley Files, Ronald Reagan Presidential Library, Simi Valley, California.

Jim Korkis, Jim. *The Unofficial Walt Disney World 1971 Companion.* Theme Park Press, 2019.

Kaufman, J. B. *South of the Border with Disney: Walt Disney and the Good Neighbor Program, 1941–1948.* Glendale, CA: Disney Editions, 2009.

Lesjack, David. *Service with Character: The Disney Studio & World War II.* Theme Park Press, 2014.

McGrory, Mary. "New Summit Will Have to Be More Than Disney World." *The Daily Item* [Port Chester, New York], July 22, 1986.

McNeil, David. "Flags of Our Fathers: Commemorating Iwo Jima." *The Asia-Pacific Journal*, January 4, 2006. https://apjjf.org/-David-McNeill/2048/article.html

Miller, Diane Disney. *The Story of Walt Disney.* New York: Henry Holt and Company, 1956.

Myers, Robert. "Mickey Mouse Returns to War-Torn Countries." *Salt Lake Telegram*, May 25, 1945.

Neild, Barry. "Mickey Mouse Brings Disney Diplomacy to Iran Theme Park." *CNN*, November 3, 2011, https://www.cnn.com/2011/11/03/world/meast/iran-roller-coasters/index.html

Nelson Rockefeller Papers. "1944–1955, Folder: Films, Walt Disney Productions. Rockefeller Archives Center, Sleepy Hollow, New York". https://dimes.rockarch.org/objects/Yirs6QfvnacZLbekSGjX4H/view

Othman, Frederick C. "Disney's Cartoon Factory All-Out For Buy A Bond, Pay a Tax Films." *The Miami Herald*, January 28, 1942.

Obama, Barack. "Remarks at Walt Disney World Resort in Lake Buena Vista, Florida." January 19, 2012. Online by Gerhard Peters and John T. Wooley, *The American Presidency Project*, http://www.presidency.ucsb.edu/ws/?pid=97562

Park, Michael K. "Long Shot: The Prospects and Limitations of Sports and Celebrity Athlete Diplomacy." *InMedia: The French Journal of Media Studies*, Vol. 6 (2017). 10.4000/inmedia.855

Pearson, Drew. "Moroccan King Western Hope." *Altoona Tribune* [Altoona, PA], December 25, 1957.

Phillips, Mark. "The Global Disney Audiences Project: Disney Across cultures." In *Dazzled by Disney? The Global Disney Audiences Project*, edited by Janet Wasko, Mark Phillips and Eileen R. Meehan, 31–61. London: Leicester University Press, 2001.

Ranta, J.S. "Disney and the Fourth." *Chicago Daily Tribune*, June 14, 1957.

Rawls, Walton. *Disney Dons Dogtags: The Best of Disney Military Insignia from World War II.* New York: The Abbeville Publishing Group, 1992.

Reynolds, Amy L. "Soviet Sailors Make Revolutionary Disney Trip." *The Orlando Sentinel*, July 18, 1991.

Rohrer, Finolo. "Back After Break." *BBC News Magazine*, June 7, 2006. http://news.bbc.co.uk/2/hi/uk_news/magazine/5054802.stm

"Saludos, Amigos, New Disney Feat of Diplomacy." *Manhattan Mercury-Chronicle* [Mercury, Kansas], November 21, 1943.

Strauss, Theodore. "Donald Duck's Disney." *New York Times*, February 7, 1943.

"Suggested Remarks for Walt Disney World." Richard Nixon Presidential Library and Museum, Yorba Linda, California. https://www.nixonlibrary.gov/sites/default/files/virtuallibrary/documents/jul11/gergen28.pdf

Thomas, Bob. *Walt Disney: An American Original*. New York: Disney Editions, 1994.

Thomas, Theodore. *Walt and El Grupo*. Film, Theodore Thomas Productions, 2008.

Tucker, George. "Manhattan The Matchbox Today." *Morning Herald* [Uniontown, PA], October 26, 1942. "TV Placement for IMV," Memo from the U.S. State Department, REF Moscow 18733, January 15, 1975. National Archives and Records Administration. https://aad.archives.gov/aad/createpdf?rid=122071&dt=2476&dl=1345

United Press International. "Disney Aide Hustled Out of Kremlin Tea." *Los Angeles Times*, June 29, 1974, p. A11.

United Press International. "Will Nikita See Disneyland? No One Seems To Know." *Tucson Daily Citizen* [Tucson, AZ], September 14, 1959.

"Weekly Highlights," Memo from the U.S. State Department, REF Tokyo 14458, October 1, 1975. National Archives and Records Administration, https://aad.archives.gov/aad/createpdf?rid=281367&dt=2476&dl=1345

Yoshimi, Sunya. "Japan: America in Japan/Japan in Disneyfication: The Disney Image and the Transformation of 'America' in Contemporary Japan." In *Dazzled by Disney? The Global Disney Audiences Project*, edited by Janet Wasko, Mark Phillips and Eileen R. Meehan, 160–181. London: Leicester University Press, 2001.

3

DISNEYLAND AND WALT DISNEY WORLD: EXPERIENCING "HISTORY" AND "IDENTITY" AT DISNEY PARKS

In 1955, Disney opened Disneyland in California, a theme park Walt Disney described in his opening speech as dedicated to "the ideals, the dreams, and the hard facts that have created America." In 1971, five years after the death of its founder, the Disney Company opened Walt Disney World in Florida, which expanded on the original template while maintaining the same basic cultural story. In building locations where people can experience simulations of historical moments alongside characters they've come to see as representations of themselves, Disney distilled the collective memories they had tapped into with their films and cartoons into a physical place. They gave a tangible form to American myths and stories of cultural identity. This distillation has turned the Disney Parks as what anthropologist Conrad Kottak has deemed an American pilgrimage location, where we travel to see "a national mythology at a sacred site."[1]

Walt Disney recognized the power of the physical to impact learning. He credited his own real-life experiences with most of his knowledge, explaining his view that "You can't force people to be scholars … There's other ways people get educated."[2] In describing Disneyland's concept Walt stated that its explicit purpose was to reach beyond the entertainment typically associated with amusement parks that were already in existence, to straddle the world between fun and learning.[3] "I don't want to just entertain kids with pony rides and slides and swings" he said, "I want them to learn something about their heritage."[4] Indeed, Walt often used the term "exhibits" when talking about his plans for Disneyland. While today we often associate the term exhibits with museums, Walt would have understood "exhibits" as also encompassing other educational and entertainment displays such as those at World's Fairs. By using the term "exhibits," Disney voiced his intention to include education as an integral part of his theme park. Taking versions of history that had already been, in Stephen Fjellman's term, "re-mythologized" in movies and television, Disney created a land where fact and

DOI: 10.4324/9781003315094-5

fiction blended together into experiences which turned into memories. Like other, more traditional living history sites such as Greenfield Village and Colonial Williamsburg, Disney theme parks offer an immersive experience of a carefully curated version of history.[5] The visitor is able to form, add to or replace their recollection of a historical moment with a lived experience. Through immediate, if recreated, experiences the stories presented in these spaces become the versions of history we most readily remember, hence, they become our collective memory.[6]

Stephen Fjellman writes that while Disney theme parks were, of course, built "by a corporation for corporate purposes" they have "transcended that corporation by assimilating and even inventing key symbols of the version of the United States" that they present.[7] Each Disney "land" within its Magic Kingdom parks contains symbols and theming evocative of the time period it displays and, by extension, the piece of the American identity it represents. Further, in each land, there are opportunities for the visitor not to simply view the past or future but to participate in it. This participatory aspect of living history and themed experiences is crucial in the formulation of the experience as collective memory.[8] The settings of each Disney "land" themselves have been well-dissected by many other scholars, with entire books, both academic and popular, devoted to the subject of Disney's land theming. The origins of the land's theming and what American traits they represent have also been covered extensively.[9] What current historiography often lacks, however, is attention to how the entirety of the themed experience in Disney's lands defines how one remembers and internalizes the location, and the connection between the theming and the association of the land with American identity traits and history in the minds of the public.

Richard Rabinowitz argues that "useful historical imagining," (a historical experience that is impactful upon its participants) has three key components: tactility (literally "the touchability of the past"), epistemology (the way "senses, words, concepts and emotions intermingle with one another in the rush of consciousness") and a sense of collaboration (visitors engaging intellectually and physically in the experience and with others around them).[10] The Disney theme parks excel in providing a version of a historical or imagined landscape that contains all three of Rabinowitz's criteria, creating spaces where the public can learn about the past in meaningful ways. This chapter discusses four Magic Kingdom lands that encompass experiences of both American history and American identity, focusing on how each land's complete experience—auditory, visual, touch and/or movement based—create lasting memories for Disney guests of both a time "remembered" and a specific aspect of a traditionally American identity.[11] These sense memories either replace or combine with other understandings of these times and themes in American history already present in the visitor, often becoming their dominant reference for that myth, event or idea. While this is not an exhaustive discussion of the vast number of experiences in each land, it is enough to illustrate how the combination of these experiences, translated into memories and paired with the symbolism and historic/mythic American influences on each land, become some of the most prominent collective memories shared by those who lay claim to identities as citizens of the United States.

FIGURE 3.1 Guide to Disneyland from 1955 showing the relationship between the themed lands and their descriptions

Source: Courtesy of the National Museum of American History, Smithsonian Institution.

Main Street, U.S.A., and Free Enterprise[12]

In Walt Disney World's Magic Kingdom and Disneyland Park in California, those memories of the United States begin with a walk down Main Street, U.S.A. More specifically, they begin with a walk up to and under the train station for Main Street, U.S.A. The train station sets the stage for the land as an homage to free enterprise, using the railroad as a symbol of new possibilities for economic growth for the small, turn-of-the-century towns the street represents. Walt Disney was particularly invested in the idea of the American small town, which many biographers have attributed to his youth in the town of Marceline, Missouri, and his disenchantment with the way of life in large urban centers (the problems of which he hoped to address with his Epcot project at the end of his life). Walt described the first land of his theme park as a result of this nostalgia.

> Many of us fondly remember our 'small hometown' and its friendly way of life at the turn of the century. To me, this era represents an important part of our heritage, and thus we have endeavored to recapture those years on Main Street, U.S.A. at Disneyland. Here is the America of 1890–1910, at the crossroads of an era … Main Street represents the typical small town in the early 1900s-the heartline of America.'[13]

As noted in Chapter 1, Walt's first cartoons often used the turn-of-the-century American small town and dignity of the common man as settings and themes; this same scenario is the one he chose to welcome guests into Disneyland. As Walt believed he himself had been a great beneficiary of the system of free enterprise, it is understandable that he used Main Street to celebrate that aspect of the American identity, both in its symbolism of economic progress, the train depot, and with its main attraction—shopping.

What the guest sees on entering Main Street is Victorian-inspired architecture, with buildings whose facades mark them as all the places one would expect to find in a small town. Right in the middle of the square as one enters is the town center, with its ceremonial flagpole and green space. To one side of the entrance is the town hall and fire house, on the other an opera house. Along the street one passes a cinema, a penny arcade, a general store/emporium, a clothier, a bakery and a soda shop. While today all the shops along Main Street on both coasts sell Disney merchandise, consumables, or Starbucks coffee, when Disneyland first opened, many of the stores were individually leased to vendors whose wares helped create a sense of small-town life, such as a Bank of America (not exactly your small-town bank, but re-presentative), an Upjohn Pharmacy, and a Ruggles China and Glass Shop.

The senses of smell and taste associated with Main Street can be summed up as "sweet." While there are restaurants that offer savory fare, the majority of the food for sale in this land is sugar-based: confectionary, bakery goods, and ice cream top the billing. The scent of Main Street consists mostly of sugar, vanilla and cinnamon. These aromas don't come solely from the bakery on the street; they are enhanced by scent machines the Disney community has dubbed "smellitzers."[14] Disney has left nothing to chance in its immersive environments, ensuring that all sensory experiences are appropriate to the land one is located in. The scent and taste of baked goods is a positive scent associated with one of the better experiences one might have in a turn-of-the-century town, visiting the baker for fresh bread and treats.

The sounds of Main Street both create and elicit fond memories in the unique setting of Disney. Background music loops play in each of the Disney Parks' themed lands, with the selections, like the scents, made with the goal of both enhancing the immersive environment and forming an associative memory. On Main Street, the music consists mainly of ragtime and swing, as well as versions of classic Disney tunes arranged in turn-of-the-century musical styles. Main Street is also one of the most frequent hosts to live music in the magic kingdom, with groups such as the Dapper Dans (a barbershop quartet) singing "Yankee Doodle Dandy," the Main Street Philharmonic (a marching band) proudly playing "Take Me Out to the Ball Game," and a ragtime pianist at Casey's Corner restaurant banging out "Maple Leaf Rag." For many guests, this music may only be experienced on Main Street, U.S.A., as it isn't prevalent in current American culture unless actively sought out. Guests may or may not enter Main Street already knowing that this music represents American popular culture of the early 1900s, but they will leave Main Street associating it with Disney's version of America in the early 1900s.

While much of the action taking place on Main Street is that of guests participating in free enterprise by making purchases, several other offerings complete the immersive environment that cements the Disney "small town" as the "American small town" in the minds of guests. Along the street, visitors can converse with the costumed "Citizens of Main Street." The Citizens include a group of suffragists, a journalist, the mayor, a fire chief, and more, who function to make guests feel as if they are a member of the small turn-of-the-century town community themselves. This sense of belonging is not only important for immersion, but also for the way it evokes the sense of the small-town population as "average citizens"—not elite politicians, wealthy bankers or academics in ivory towers but the "common man" so often vaunted by Walt Disney and others as the backbone of the nation. Guests are invited to participate in other "small town" activities as well, such as lowering the American flag in town square at the end of every day or riding a horse-drawn trolley to the end of the street.

At Disneyland Park, Main Street's Opera House houses Great Moments with Mr. Lincoln, where the president's audio-animatronic figure has delivered excerpts of some of his most famous speeches multiple times a day for over 50 years. Upon the attraction's opening in 1966 (it had debuted at the 1964 World's Fair), a reviewer noted "Visitors actually feel themselves present at one of Lincoln's speeches. And at Disneyland 'Great Moments with Mr. Lincoln' becomes an even more memorable experience because of its surroundings in the Opera House just off Disneyland's Town Square."[15] The reviewer noted that the visitor stepped into a room reminiscent of a Victorian-era White House, complete with a picture window showing Washington, D.C. Moving directly from the town square and into Lincoln's speeches provides an effect reminiscent of a president stopping at a small town on a whistle-stop tour, politicking, and then moving to the next location. The visitor dips into the national moment, viewing one of the handful of presidents who have become almost nonpartisan national icons, then returns to the daily life of "their" town. The attraction speaks to the national character in ways that resonated not just in 1966, but in 1990. When rumors began to circulate that Lincoln was going to be replaced with a Muppet-themed attraction, the public outcry was enough to cause park operators to cancel the planned closure. "This exhibit carries a message to the people of the United States. It's something very emotional" said one visitor, while a show hostess reported people coming to her in tears over the prospect of its closure.[16] The theater in Anaheim, California, is one of the only places for the American public to encounter the Great Emancipator in what is as close to the flesh as they can get, and its existence, and that experience, has become important to them.

Former Executive Vice President of Walt Disney Entertainment Ron Logan summed up the impact of experiencing the activities of Main Street in person. "I was in the Magic Kingdom and heard the Dapper Dans sing live … I felt like I was experiencing it in 'real time' but 'real time' of the past."[17] The line between past and present is blurred here, and one can truly feel as if they have visited the American small town of the national narrative. Even though it never truly existed as it may live in the collective memory, it exists in tangible form at the Disney theme parks, and that is real enough.

Main Street, like the rest of Disneyland, is "truer to our national collective unconscious than our actual history, bespotted with its social turmoil."[18] Main Street is full of promise—the train has just arrived, the business owners on Main Street (as portrayed by the Citizens) are excited to welcome new customers and in turn their own prosperity. The storefronts are still shiny and new, no potholes mar the streets. The family-run shops have yet to be run out of business by national chains.[19] The Citizens of Main Street might have some disagreements (the suffragists are often found campaigning against the current mayor, for instance), but they speak in jest and still come together to sing, laugh, and gossip, and there are no questions or concerns about who has access to citizenship. Absent are any unpleasant stenches one may also have found in the 19th-century small town, such as horse manure. Not only is the visitor experiencing a "typical turn-of-the-century American town," but they are experiencing only the very best version of such a town, making the memory associated with it a pleasant one—one more likely for Americans to want to claim as part of their identity than, say, a small town going to seed because its occupants are all moving to the nearest city and its businesses are failing. On Main Street, free enterprise equals prosperity equals American small town equals the wafting scent of baked goods equals happiness. Main Street is the idealized version of our collective past on which we build our current identity. Through its sensory experiences, it becomes implanted in our individual and then collective consciousness, becoming the archetype for "the American main street."[20] Its foundational American myths—the ultimate triumph of free enterprise, the dignity of the small-town, average American—set the stage for the rest of the Magic Kingdom and Disneyland Park as a continued journey into American history and experiences.

Frontierland and Rugged Individualism

At the end of Main Street stands Sleeping Beauty Castle (in Disneyland) or Cinderella Castle (in Walt Disney World). From this point, guests can choose to enter one of the several lands arranged in a radial around the castle hub. This tour now takes the second left at the hub after Main Street, which at Disneyland Park brings the guest to a version of the rugged individualism personified by the Wild West in Frontierland (Walt Disney World visitors will first pass through Liberty Square before encountering Frontierland). Theming here echoes a movie-set vision of the American "Old West", and where Davy Crockett and Pecos Bill would be at home among saloons, desert pines and mine trains, all neatly symbolized by the coonskin caps still sold in the gift shops there.[21] In a 1964 guide to Disneyland, Walt was quoted describing how he saw the land and its purpose: "Here you can return to Frontier America. All these and many other adventures in Frontierland are designed to give you the feeling of having 'lived,' even for a short while, during our country's days of pioneer development."[22] For Walt Disney and other political conservatives of the 1950s, the frontier was considered the absolute embodiment of the "American Spirit," a signifier of individual freedom, of the pull-yourself-up-by-your-bootstraps rugged individualism that paved the way to individual and national success.[23] Frontierland is a physical embodiment of Frederick Jackson Turner's frontier thesis that held that the American character was forged in its western expansion, through subduing the frontier's lands and peoples, through struggle and survival. At the Disney theme parks, Frontierland is designed to give visitors a sense of having lived that struggle without having to struggle in any real sense at all.

Frontierland offers many attractions where the guest can take action to become part of the experience. They can ride a mine train, where their point of view is that of a miner, echoing the sense of America as a place of "common men," rather than say, a wealthy mine owner. This association with the common man is reinforced when guests take a log raft to Tom Sawyer Island, where they can playact as Mark Twain's Tom Sawyer and Huck Finn in a "frontier fort" and then return to stomp their feet and clap their hands in the rustic frontier hall setting of the Country Bear Jamboree (in Walt Disney World). After their "work" in the mine, guests can relax and take in a show at the Golden Horseshoe Saloon (in Disneyland) or take aim with a .54-caliber Hawkins buffalo rifle and fire at targets in a recreation of Boot Hill, Tombstone, Arizona, in the Frontierland Shootin' Arcade. Guests might board a riverboat to tour the "Rivers of America," paddle around in one of Davy Crockett's Explorer Canoes (formerly the Indian War Canoes) or stop at a "trading post" to purchase leather goods or comestibles for their "journey." In the early years of Disneyland, guests could even tour the rugged landscape by Conestoga wagon or on the back of a pack mule.

Taking up a place next to the Rivers of America allows the guest to fully take in the sights, as well as the scents, sounds and potentially tastes, of Disney's frontier. The whistle of the riverboat functions like a siren call to head deeper down the river, to the next frontier. Banjo and blue grass folk tunes mix with birdsongs and water lapping on the "river's" shore, epitomizing the confluence (or conflict) of nature and humankind in a place where "wild" is conceivably being "tamed." In the distance a train whistle sounds, a reminder that somewhere behind you exists "civilization," towns, and modern amenities, even as your eyes perceive only roughhewn wood structures alongside the wild river's shores, an auditory way of placing the guest on the precipice of the frontier. In the air wafts a distinct mix of scents: roasted spiced nuts, popcorn, turkey legs, wood, smoke and leather goods. The roasted meat, wood, smoke and leather scents may bring to mind some of the symbols associated with the frontier today: campfires, horse saddles, wood-burning stoves, while the turkey legs and popcorn add a distinctively "Disney" scent to the experience. The scent of Frontierland, then, is both evocative of a historic time and place and simultaneously extant only on Disney property, connecting both in the guest's mind. These cues are then associated with memories of the essence of Frontierland when experienced outside the parks as well. A student writing for a Disney blog recalled "I walked through a nearby courtyard multiple times before being able to place its smell to the rustic ruggedness of Frontierland (it was finally a live banjo player that got me the connection)."[24]

Frontierland is important in the American collective memory not just for how it shapes the way guests visualize the American frontier and the American spirit that it embodies, but for the way in which it offers a place to celebrate and remember American folk heroes whose narratives either lack physical locations to visit or whose locations of memory are scattered vastly across the United States. In one day, guests can pay homage to the folk vision of Mark Twain and his characters on Tom Sawyer Island and the Mark Twain Riverboat in Disneyland Park, to the idealized Davy Crockett established in Disney's films on "his" canoes at Disneyland and in singing along with *The Ballad of Davy Crockett* at the Country Bear Jamboree at Disney World. Pecos Bill has his own Tall Tale Inn and Café. While other locations of remembering these folk heroes do exist (notably the Mark Twain Boyhood Home and Museum in Hannibal, Missouri, and the Davy Crockett Cabin-Museum in Rutherford, Tennessee), their existence together at the Disney Parks concentrates their resonance as symbols of the American frontier. Their existence in Frontierland also emphasizes the legitimacy of Frontierland as representative of the American west as America has mythologized it. During the Crockett craze, the magazine *Colliers* wrote "'who can say that Daniel Boone is any more real an American hero than Pecos Bill or Paul Bunyan or Huckleberry Finn? It is [the one doing the idolizing] who makes the hero real."[25] And yet, like the frontier town that is no longer real, that never was exactly as it is remembered today, those American heroes *do* exist, not just in the American imagination, but at the Disney Parks.

As the less positive aspects of small-town life go unportrayed on Main Street, the unsavory aspects of the frontier are largely absent from Frontierland. While fortifications and stockade stylings hint at a defensive posture, they don't allude to whom (or what) the pioneers might have had reason to fear. American Indian presence is relegated to audio-animatronic figures along the Rivers of America (this is discussed further in later chapters). There is no sense of how perilous frontier life could be, hence the feeling associated with it is a wholly positive one, reinforcing the sense that rugged individualism and America's historic frontier are essentially "good," and thus a positive part of the American character.

FIGURE 3.2 Souvenir map of Walt Disney World's Magic Kingdom from 1973 showing Liberty Square

Source: Courtesy of the National Museum of American History, Smithsonian Institution.

Liberty Square and Independence

If the Disney guests are in Florida, they pass from Frontierland into a vision of America on the verge of revolution in Liberty Square. For the full symbolic experience, however, they would enter not from Frontierland but from the castle hub over a bridge representative of Concord's North Bridge, the site of the "shot heard 'round the world" that began the American Revolutionary War. On the bridge, the visitors symbolically and literally cross over into another time period. Described in Disney's official history of Walt Disney World from that park's 50th anniversary in 2021, Liberty Square "presents a panorama of the times (pre- and post-American Revolution), locales, and architectural styles-that range from the Dutch New Amsterdam designs of New York to the Georgian style of Virginia, the Federal influences of Philadelphia, and to the New England character of Massachusetts." The book emphasizes that the experience in Liberty Square triggers "a nostalgia for an era they never experienced but are aware of from educational and entertainment sources."[26]

In Liberty Square, the small visual details that pull from the educational reference points of children schooled in the United States are particularly effective at triggering an emotional connection between the visitor and the national narrative. Symbols sprinkled throughout the colonial architecture reference key foundational myths the current national narrative ascribes to. Two lanterns in a window in one building intentionally call to mind the signal placed in the Old North Church in Boston for Paul Revere to warn the Americans of the arrival of British forces.[27] A replica of the Liberty Bell in Philadelphia, cast from the same mold as the original, is surrounded by flags of the 13 original colonies.[28] At the center of the square stands a "Liberty Tree," representative of the one made famous in Boston. Nearby signage, designed to look like a pamphlet tacked up illegally by the Sons of Liberty, encouraging "Every Friend of his country, to Himself, and to Posterity" to "meet under the Liberty Tree at IX o'Clock to oppose the machinations of Tyranny."[29]

While standing at the Liberty Tree guests are serenaded with music that speaks to the time and identity of Liberty Square. Music that was popular in the United States in the late 1700s was recorded for the land's background loops using time-period-appropriate instruments such as the harpsichord, violin and fife.[30] Yet anachronistically, over time music has been included that is associated with American patriotism, such as military or patriotic marches ythat are not of the revolutionary time period, such as "You're a Grand Old Flag" and "Stars and Stripes Forever."[31] These are played in service of associating the land with traditional forms of patriotism, an example of the ideals communicated by the land taking precedent over their historical accuracy.

The tastes and smells of Liberty Square are less "of the time period" than "of their restaurants," which are themselves places meant to locate the visitor in Revolutionary America. The scent of funnel cake, for instance, a treat not invented until the 1950s, leads the visitor to a quick service food stop called Sleepy Hollow, where an open kitchen allows guests to see cast in colonial costume preparing their treats in a building modeled on the home of America's first home-grown internationally bestselling author, Washington Irving.[32] The scent and taste of seafood, appropriate for a setting evoking a New England seaport, centers the visitor on Colombia Harbor House, themed as the interior of a 19th-century sailing vessel, and the taste of a "traditional" Thanksgiving dinner can be found in the Liberty Tree Tavern, created to mimic the public taverns where America's founders met, drank, and discussed revolution. Notably absent is any human waste stench stemming from the sewage tossed out of the windows of colonial homes in the days before indoor plumbing, though these rivers of waste are represented graphically on the ground with brown-colored pathways in Liberty Square.[33]

The participatory aspects of Liberty Square emphasize the role of the average citizen in the creation of America's democracy. The anchor attraction of Liberty Square is the Hall of Presidents. Here visitors come face to face with audio-animatronic versions of each president and watch a presentation on the history of the United States and its government. The attraction itself is a hagiographic homage to the elite men who have held the position of president of the United

States. However, the simple fact that the visitor can come physically close to these presidential proxies, who will then perform for the visitor, is a reminder that the president is, at least in theory, a servant to the people. In Disney World, the avatar of the president is summoned solely for the enjoyment of guests. The presence of personal artifacts from several presidents, on loan from museums around the country, in the preshow area of the attraction lends credibility both to the location as representative of America in some official capacity, and to the idea that the president, down to his material artifacts on display, belongs directly to the people.

Today guest interaction with historical figures in the rest of Liberty Square is mostly limited to watching reenactments of foundational Revolutionary myths as portrayed by the Muppets in "The Muppets Present ... Great Moments in American History." The interactive show is a light-hearted exercise in the "collective" participation in a collective memory. During each show, the Muppets retell, with much comedic flair, an important story from early American history, currently either the midnight ride of Paul Revere or the signing of the Declaration of Independence. During the show recounting the Declaration of Independence signing, an actor on the ground occasionally engages the audience who are encouraged to pretend to be part of the historical scene being presented, providing guests with a common cultural experience. The show also features a cast member who acts as a town crier, which is reminiscent of the early experiences that gave the land so much of its colonial character, but which no longer exist. At varying times since 1971, there has been in Liberty Square a town crier who told guests of the day's news, appearances by Benjamin Franklin and Betsy Ross, and a fife and drum corps who would conduct a daily ceremony, "Sons and Daughters of Liberty," during which they would induct two children into their revolutionary ranks.[34] These types of interactions, like those with the Citizens of Main Street, helped to establish the setting of the land and envelop guests within its environment as if they were truly experiencing revolutionary America.

Liberty Square transports the visitor to a formative time in American history, and on the way emphasizes themes integral to "American character," particularly independence and the triumph of the common man and underdog. Reminding guests of the contributions of the Sons of Liberty alongside those of the presidents emphasizes the equal worth of both in the American narrative. Centering the square around the Liberty Tree places the common person's role in the revolution at the forefront of the experience in ways that even the official sites of memory failed, at least initially, to do. For example, in the 1770s the tree represented a meeting place where no social or economic gatekeeping made citizens feel unwelcome, as coffee houses or even taverns might. The tree was where "petty tradesmen, laborers, and women who were shut out of the Colony's decision-making but became a vocal, driving, unavoidable force for change."[35] The original Liberty Tree having been cut down by the British shortly after the war began, its site was largely ignored by later locals and historians alike, left out of Boston's Freedom Trail and official histories as a way, Alfred F. Young suggests, for the elite to foster a "willful forgetting" of the common man's role. Today the original site of the tree in Boston is marked only by a plaque, but in Walt Disney World, guests can literally gather underneath it, where another plaque informs them of its place in history.[36] Guests leave Liberty Square with the impression of a fiercely independent nation where the common revolutionary man is just as important as the president of the United States, an idea they take with them after they leave the park as they continually reform their collective identity.

Tomorrowland and Conquering New Frontiers

Crossing from one side of the park to the other, guests cross temporally from the past and into the future. Tomorrowland has undergone many changes over the years, but at its heart has remained themed around the idea that Americans have the opportunity, the duty even, to conquer new and greater frontiers and to continue a forward march of progress. This ideal is represented in this land by the idea of space travel and other technological advancements—new frontiers of science.[37] The plaque at the entrance to Tomorrowland in Disneyland is inscribed with Walt's description of the land as a place that "offers new frontiers in science, adventure and ideals: the Atomic Age ... the challenge of outer space ... and the hope for a peaceful and unified world." Walt's words were delivered in 1955, but they sound an awful lot like Kennedy's description of America's new frontier 15 years later. When accepting the Democratic Party's nomination as their presidential candidate for 1960, Kennedy declared that Americans were standing on the edge of a "New Frontier" with its "uncharted territories of science and space," that would test the American character anew, as the "old" frontier had done, to "prove all over again whether this nation ... can long endure" (and, of course, "compete with the single-minded advance of the Communist system.")[38] Like Kennedy's vision for America, Tomorrowland is both a product of the time in which it was conceived and the ideals its creators subscribed to. Though the exact experiences there have changed over time, the land still effectively communicates those ideals into guests' collective memory.[39]

Physical experiences in Tomorrowland center largely on forms of transportation. Once, there was the Rocket to the Moon, which simulated a launch into space before that was a reality even for an astronaut, much less for those with the means to purchase a ticket on a private rocket, as can happen today (though Walt Disney did presciently say of the attraction that it would be "a thrilling preview of a space voyage that many Americans may live to make.")[40] While the Rocket to the Moon no longer exists, there is Space Mountain, a perennially popular dark roller coaster ride that zooms guests through space in a small rocket. Actual transportation in the park supported this theme. The monorail and PeopleMover attractions allowed guests to participate in Walt's vision of what future transportation might someday be like in their own towns.[41] While they seem less futuristic today than they did in 1955, the Autopia cars (Tomorrowland Speedway at Walt Disney World), allowed guests to experience a simulation of a freeway, which was a brand-new idea in 1955 (the Federal-Aid Highway Act, which funded the creation of most interstate highways, wouldn't be signed until 1956). Various exhibits of new and potential future technologies came and went in the park: the Monsanto House of the Future, a Hall of Chemistry, exhibits on Dutch Boy Paint and the future of dairy farming, a flying saucer ride and a walkaround "spaceman," all of which blended together the idea of both space and technology as new frontiers for guests to experience.[42] To this day at Walt Disney World, the Carousel of Progress, a rotating stage show depicting better living through technological progress over time, takes visitors through time periods in American history as well as a time in a theoretical future. It emphasizes the importance of both Americans' willingness to try new technologies (taking steps into new frontiers) and the comfort that technology offers to everyday life, ensuring that guests leave the experience associating those new frontiers with a collective "good" for both the individual and for the country at large.[43]

The scents of Tomorrowland are unique in the sense that there are few other cultural referents to what "tomorrow" should smell like. They consist mainly of scents generated by or on the land's rides. The Autopia/Tomorrowland Speedway attraction provides Tomorrowland with one of its most distinct scents: gasoline. While it isn't a scent every guest might describe as pleasant, it is distinctive to the land and evocative of the theme of movement in its association with gas-powered vehicles. The other defining scent of Tomorrowland is Disney's version of "space." The interior of Space Mountain represents first a space port and then the dark void of space itself. A popular candle sold by a maker unaffiliated with Disney describes the scent of the ride they attempt to capture with their candle as that of "bergamot, crisp air and cold steel ... blue lavender, watercrest [sic] and heliotrope ... grey musk, sandalwood and iron asteroid."[44] Most Disney guests have never had the opportunity to smell space itself, nor the interior of a space rocket. Nevertheless, they do have a scent that they associate with space travel-and it comes from the Disney Parks.

All of the guests' senses are engaged in this land. Today most of the tastes of Tomorrowland involve standard theme park fare: popcorn, hotdogs, cheeseburgers, etc. One popular Tomorrowland treat, ice cream, does have ties to a defunct futuristic exhibit. The Dairy Bar opened in Tomorrowland at Disneyland in 1956, serving glasses of milk, described as "nature's most perfect food" to guests after they had toured an exhibit about the future of dairy in America, including "flying deliverymen, high-tech nutritional milk, and state-of-the-art milking technology."[45] The sounds of Tomorrowland, too, may seem like standard "futuristic" varieties today, but they reference the collective memory of science fiction films and "new age" styles of music to suggest the future, heavily using synthesizers and sound effects to differentiate from the music found in other park areas. As Claire Nat noted for Disney travel blog touringplans.com, it is the combination of the "science fiction" style music, which exists in the collective consciousness before a guest's arrival, with the sounds of "action" taking place in the land that truly locate the visitor in a new frontier soundscape. Nat notes, "Whether it's the mechanical sounds of the arms that lift the Astro Orbiter's ships or the smooth hum of the Tomorrowland Transit Authority PeopleMover units passing by, all the extra sounds of Tomorrowland actually *blend* with the sound-track," creating a unique auditory experience of America's potential new frontiers not found anywhere else.[46]

Conclusion

All of these images, scents, sounds, tastes and experiences, these snapshots of time specifically engineered to be pleasant and conflict free, based on Disney's cartoon work and his personal, intensely patriotic vision of American history, loom large in the collective memories of millions of American citizens, not to mention many international visitors. The settings of these "lands" provide a physical space not just for the understanding of American history but also, as we will see later, the negotiation of what constitutes the American identity and experience at any given time.

Of course, the images from Main Street, Frontierland, Liberty Square and Tomorrowland do not sit alone in our collective memory. At Walt Disney World, Epcot provides additional locations that emphasize the themes of liberty, patriotism and progress at Epcot. Future World, one half of the park, is completely devoted to technological innovation and the expansion of horizons both physical (such as in the park's attraction Mission Space, where visitors can crew a mission to Mars) and intellectual (the park's most physically imposing attraction, Spaceship Earth, details the history and potential future of better living through science and discovery). In the central pavilion in Epcot's World Showcase, known as the American Adventure, visitors are immersed in detailed colonial theming and can enjoy a theater show hosted by Audio-Animatronic figures of Benjamin Franklin and Mark Twain. American symbols in their own right, Franklin and Twain present a sweeping overview of American history focusing on stories widely recognized as having a role in making up the American identity. These include defining moments of struggle such as the Civil War and Great Depression that Americans now look back to with an eye for what moral lessons they have to impart. Disneyland now boasts Disney California Adventure Park, where lands such as Hollywoodland and Grizzly Peak act, much like the Hollywood Studios and Animal Kingdom parks do at Walt Disney World, to create a lived experience of old Hollywood, where so many American myths were concretized in film, and to explore themes of rugged outdoor adventure in both American and foreign landscapes and ecology, respectively. Ecology is also touched on in the American Adventure through a vignette showing John Muir and Teddy Roosevelt planning national parks.

The feelings of excitement, adventure, patriotism, progress, etc. elicited through the sensory experiences in each of these lands bind for the visitor to the place and symbols with which they were experienced, while also being associated with the history they evoke, and they will be inextricably entwined in our memories. If being an American means to be full of excitement, liberty, adventure, and patriotism, then the places that can evoke all of those feelings in one day while using American cultural stories must, it would follow in our memory, be integral to understanding what being an American means. They must in fact be a part of the American identity.

Notes

1 Conrad Kottak quoted in Peter Carlson, "More Real than Reality," *Washington Post,* May 15, 1994, BB11.
2 As told to Peter Martin and Diane Disney Miller in 1956, quoted in Steven Watts, *The Magic Kingdom: Walt Disney and the American Way of Life* (Columbia, MO: University of Missouri Press, 1997), 13.
3 Amusement parks had been in existence in the United States since the opening of Lake Compounce in Bristol, Connecticut, in 1846. The idea of pleasure gardens had existed in Europe long before that. Walt Disney visited many theme and amusement parks gathering ideas for Disneyland, including Griffith Park, Knott's Berry Farm, Tivoli Gardens, Colonial Williamsburg and Greenfield Village. Walt is often quoted as differentiating his park from others because of his attention to cleanliness, creating places where families could partake of amusements together, and offering both an educational and entertaining experience. For amusement park history see Barry Hill, *Imagineering an American Dreamscape: Genesis, Evolution, and Redemption of the Regional Theme Park* (Cary, IL: Rivershore Creative, 2020); Stephen M. Silverman, *The Amusement Park: 900 Years of Thrills and Spills, and the Dreamers and Schemers Who Built Them* (New York: Black Dog & Leventhal Publishers, 2019).
4 Karal Ann Marling, "Disneyland, 1955: Just Take the Santa Ana Freeway to the American Dream," *American Art* 5, no. ½ (Winter-Spring 1991): 173, https://doi.org/10.1086/424113.
5 Walt Disney visited both locations several times before opening Disneyland.
6 Amy Levin describes attractions such as Colonial Williamsburg and Greenfield Village as places "where public history may be transformed into collective memory as visitors come to remember the experience of visiting the site rather than 'pure' history," a descriptor that can also be aptly applied to the Disney Parks. Amy K. Levin, ed., *Defining Memory: Local Museums and the Construction of History in America's Changing Communities* (Lanham, MD: AltaMira Press, 2007), 45. See also Richard Handler and Eric Gable, *The New History in an Old Museum: Creating the Past at Colonial Williamsburg* (Durham: Duke University Press, 1997).
7 Stephen Fjellman, *Vinyl Leaves: Walt Disney World and America* (Boulder, CO: Westview Press, 1992), 21.
8 Scott Bukatman dissects how the fully immersive experiences at Disney transform the "real spatial movement of the spectator" into "a simulated temporal trajectory," that is a sense of true travel in time and space. Bukatman describes the experience: "What finally occurs through all of the intensification of sensory experience on the rides … is nothing less than an inscription of the body, on the body. These journeys into technologically complex zones ultimately serve to guarantee the continuing presence and relevance of the subject. You have a body, the rides announce, you exist. The body, and thus the subject, penetrates these impossible spaces, finally to merge with them in a state of kinetic, sensory pleasure. The visitor is thus projected into the datascape, and is incorporated by the technology quite as fully as the cyberspace cowboys of Neuromancer. The inscription on the body announces the human-machine interface, and technology thereby creates the conditions for its own acceptance". Scott Bukatman, "There's Always Tomorrowland: Disney and the Hypercinematic Experience," *October*, Vol. 57 (Summer, 1991): 75–77.
9 Margaret J. King, Stephen Fjellman and Karal Ann Marling, to name a few, have done overviews of the symbolism and values in the parks as a whole. See in particular

Richard Francaviglia, "Main Street U.S.A.: A Comparison/Contrast of Streetscapes in Disneyland and Walt Disney World," *The Journal of Popular Culture*, Vol. 15, Issue 1 (Summer 1981): 141–156, as well as Francaviglia, "Walt Disney's Frontierland as an Allegorical Map of the American West," *Western Historical Quarterly*, Vol. 30, No. 2 (Summer, 1999): 155–182, and David Johnson, "Disney World as Structure and Symbol: Re-Creation of the American Experience," *The Journal of Popular Culture*, Vol. 15, Issue 1 (Summer 1981): 157–165. A useful discussion of each land at Disneyland can be found in Priscilla Hobbs, *Walt's Utopia: Disneyland and American Mythmaking* (Jefferson, NC: McFarland & Company, Inc., Publishers, 2015).

10 Richard Rabinowitz, *Curating America: Journeys Through Storyscapes of the American Past* (Chapel Hill, NC: The University of North Carolina Press, 2016), 29.

11 While every themed land in both Disneyland Park and Walt Disney World's Magic Kingdom has something to offer the guest in terms of American identity, for purposes of brevity this chapter will focus on those that were both present on either park's opening day and are tied most explicitly to the American narrative. Using this metric, I omit Adventureland and Fantasyland from both parks, as well as New Orleans Square, Critter Country and Star Wars Land from Disneyland Park. The omission of lands opened after opening day is simply a way to narrow focus. The omission of Adventureland and Fantasyland is to allow more space for those lands that most embody the American identity through their physical experiences. Adventureland and Fantasyland are both tied to American identity in that Adventureland reflects a colonialist mindset and an othering of nonwhite races and Fantasyland is tied to white European immigration in its use of Old-World fairy tales, but this connection is much more subtle than the blatant historical theming of Frontierland or new frontier rhetoric of Tomorrowland. Later chapters will, however, discuss how changes to attractions in Adventureland and Critter Country have played a part in the negotiation of American identity at the Disney Parks.

12 There are differences, both subtle and great, between the experiences and lands as they exist at Walt Disney World and Disneyland. The lands and experiences have changed over time as well. This section does not aim to catalog those differences or changes, but rather takes a wide lens view of the lands' overall themes, highlighting certain experiences, not to suggest that they exist in the same exact way over space and time but to give a sense of the overall experience visitors may have had regardless of what decade they came in or which coast they visited. All of the touches and attractions discussed were present in the early years of the parks and are present in some form today, unless noted otherwise.

13 Walt Disney quoted in Watts, *The Magic Kingdom*, 22.

14 Scientific research has shown that the part of the brain involved in scent processing is also a key part for the formation of long-term memories, particularly among groups—an important piece of collective memory. Scent is an important aspect of Disney nostalgia within the Disney community, so much so that many individual vendors now sell candles, wax melts, and room sprays designed to smell like different places in the parks. See sites such as "Science of Disney: Smellitizers," *ThePhDPrincess,* https://phdprincess.com/blog/disney-smells, accessed January 31, 2022, or Darren Wittko, "Walt Disney World Behind the Magic: Smellitzer Machines," *OrlandoParksGuy.com*, April 27, 2020, https://orlandoparksguy.com/blog/2020/4/26/ walt-disney-world-behind-the-magic-smellitzer-machines. National Science Teacher's Association, "Emotion and Scent," *The Science Teacher*, Vol. 75, no. 9 (December 2008): 18.

15 Kermit Holt, "First Color Photo of Disney's 'Mr. Lincoln'" *Chicago Tribune*, July 31, 1966, 6.

16 Bob Pool, "Lincoln Liberated," *Los Angeles Times*, August 24, 1990, 3.

17 Jim Korkis, "WDW Chronicles: The Music of Main Street, U.S.A.," *All Ears*, March 19, 2013, https://allears.net/wdw-chronicles-the-music-of-main-street-u-s-a/.

18 Douglas Brode, *Multiculturalism and the Mouse: Race and Sex in Disney Entertainment (Austin: University of Texas Press, 2006),* 256.

19 The replacement of individually leased shops by Disney-owned stores on Main Street mirrors this historical trend, though the original lessees were in general established, successful businesses, not exactly mom and pop shops.

20 See Richard Francaviglia's excellent examination of Disney's influence on ideas of "Main Street, U.S.A." in Francaviglia, *Main Street Revisited Time, Space, and Image Building in Small-Town America* (Iowa City: University of Iowa Press, 1996).

21 Frontierland almost seamlessly blends "fictional myth," such as Pecos Bill, an entirely invented folk hero, with "the historical mythological," such as the idealized version of true historic figure Davy Crockett. Credit for the quoted terms goes to Claire Jerry.

22 Walt Disney quoted in Marcy Carriker Smothers, *Walt's Disneyland: A Walk in the Park with Walt Disney* (Los Angeles: Disney Editions, 2021), 84.

23 Francaviglia, "Allegory," 167.

24 Blake Taylor, "Extraordinary Magic in Everyday Life," *WDWRadio,* May 1, 2013, https://www.wdwradio.com/2013/05/finding-disney-hidden-disney-smells/.

25 *Colliers* quoted in "Walt and the King of the Wild Frontier," *The Walt Disney Family Museum,* August 17, 2011, https://www.waltdisney.org/blog/walt-and-king-wild-frontier.

26 Kevin Kern, Tim O'Day and Steven Vagnini, *A Portrait of Walt Disney World: 50 Years of the Most Magical Place on Earth* (Los Angeles: Disney Editions, 2021), 95.

27 Made famous by Henry Wadsworth Longfellow in his poem, "Paul Revere's Ride," where Paul Revere received a signal telling him how the British were arriving with lantern numbers—"one if by land, two if by sea."

28 Gene Duncan, "Let Freedom Ring on Independence Day," *Disney Parks Blog,* July 4, 2010, https://disneyparks.disney.go.com/blog/2010/07/let-freedom-ring-on-independence-day/.

29 The Liberty Tree was a potent symbol of revolt in revolutionary America, the story of which is neatly summed up by Erick Trickey, "The Story Behind a Forgotten Symbol of the American Revolution: The Liberty Tree," *Smithsonian Magazine,* May 19, 2016, https://www.smithsonianmag.com/history/story-behind-forgotten-symbol-american-revolution-liberty-tree-180959162/. The Sons of Liberty was a loosely formed underground revolutionary group active in the Boston Tea Party and Stamp Act protests.

30 Claire Nat, "Magic Kingdom AtMousePhere: The Music of Liberty Square," *Touring Plans,* August 16, 2014, https://touringplans.com/blog/magic-kingdom-atmousephere-music-liberty-square/.

31 For a list of background music in Liberty Square over time, see "The Music of Liberty Square, 1980-Now," *Passport to Dreams,* January 22, 2018, http://passport2dreams.blogspot.com/2016/05/the-music-of-liberty-square-1980-now.html.

32 While the outline of the home is similar, some of the detailing has been changed to better fit with the colonial theming and coloring of the land. Readers may note that Irving was not a colonial author, but rather an author of early America; his inclusion here is meant to illustrate the way the land celebrates uniquely American heroes and traits, of which Irving is one. His inclusion is also illustrative of the way in which Disney will play with historical facts to serve the identity of their space. "The 'Sunnyside' of Sleepy Hollow," *Disney Parks Blog,* July 8, 2010, https://disneyparks.disney.go.com/blog/2010/07/the-sunnyside-of-sleepy-hollow/.

33 Most guests are unaware of this detail, as it isn't called out directly in the park. Brian McDaniel, *Walt Disney World: The Full Report* (Bloomington, IN: iUniverse, 2008), 96.

34 See Jim Korkis, "WDW Chronicles: Year One-Liberty Square 1971," *All Ears,* September 20, 2011, https://allears.net/wdw-chronicles-year-one-liberty-square-1971/.

35 Brian MacQuarrie, "Liberty Tree Protest 250 Years Ago Is Marked," *Boston Globe,* August 14, 2015, https://www.bostonglobe.com/metro/2015/08/14/the-liberty-tree-long-gone-and-mostly-forgotten-marks-birthday/pFEXczClYeC4TIKlYdIiEK/story.html.

36 Alfred Young quoted in Trickey, "The Story Behind."

37 Scott Bukatman sums up the visual esthetic of the land well: "While in Tomorrowland, each aerodynamically turned, turquoise- and-white-colored detail enshrines a visible yearning for flight, a thrusting beyond limits, and the hope and confidence in an un-ambivalently better tomorrow." Bukatman, "There's always," 3.

38 John F. Kennedy, "The New Frontier," acceptance speech of Senator John F. Kennedy, Democratic National Convention, 15 July 1960, John F. Kennedy Presidential Library and Museum, Boston, MA, digitized at https://www.jfklibrary.org/asset-viewer/archives/JFKSEN/0910/JFKSEN-0910-015, 6–7.

39 See Sabrina Mittermeyer, *A Cultural History of the Disneyland Theme Parks: Middle Class Kingdoms (Chicago: Intellect Books, 2021).*

40 Walt Disney quoted in Smothers, *Walt's Disneyland*, 134.

41 The PeopleMover no longer exists at Disneyland, but its Disney World cousin, the Tomorrowland Transit Authority, is the author's personal favorite Magic Kingdom experience.

42 An excellent compendium of Tomorrowland attractions through the years (and of Disney attractions over the years generally) can be found at davelandweb.com/disneyland.

43 The Carousel of Progress originated as "Progressland" at the 1964 World's Fair, sponsored by General Electric. It was then exhibited at Disneyland and moved to Walt Disney World in 1975, where it has run ever since, with occasional updates. The video shown to guests before entering the attraction emphasizes that it is "America's longest running stage show" with the most performances of any theater show in the country.

44 Magic Candle Company, "Space Coaster" candle description, accessed February 7, 2022, https://magiccandlecompany.com/collections/frontpage/products/space-coaster?ref=popsugar.com.

45 "Dairy Bar," *Duchess of Disneyland*, October 22, 2015, https://duchessofdisneyland.com/park-history/dairy-bar/.

46 Claire Nat, "Magic Kingdom AtMousePhere: Tomorrowland Music," *Touring Plans Blog*, July 21, 2014, accessed February 8, 2022. https://touringplans.com/blog/magic-kingdom-tomorrowland-music/.

References

Brode, Douglas. *Multiculturalism and the Mouse: Race and Sex in Disney Entertainment*. Austin: University of Texas Press, 2006.

Bukatman, Scott. "There's always Tomorrowland: Disney and the Hypercinematic Experience." *October*, Vol. 57 (Summer, 1991): 55–78.

Carlson, Peter. "More Real than Reality." *Washington Post*, May 15, 1994.

"Dairy Bar." *Duchess of Disneyland*, October 22, 2015. https://duchessofdisneyland.com/park-history/dairy-bar/

Duncan, Gene. "Let Freedom Ring on Independence Day," *Disney Parks Blog*, July 4, 2010, https://disneyparks.disney.go.com/blog/2010/07/let-freedom-ring-on-independence-day/

Fjellman, Stephen. *Vinyl Leaves: Walt Disney World and America*. Boulder, CO: Westview Press, 1992.

Francaviglia, Richard. "Main Street U.S.A.: A Comparison/Contrast of Streetscapes in Disneyland and Walt Disney World," *The Journal of Popular Culture*, Vol. 15, Issue 1 (Summer 1981): 141–156.

Francaviglia, Richard. "Walt Disney's Frontierland as an Allegorical Map of the American West," *Western Historical Quarterly*, Vol. 30, No. 2 (Summer, 1999): 155–182

Francaviglia, Richard. *Main Street Revisited Time, Space, and Image Building in Small-Town America*. Iowa City: University of Iowa Press, 1996.

Handler, Richard and Eric Gable. *The New History in an Old Museum: Creating the Past at Colonial Williamsburg*. Durham: Duke University Press, 1997.

Hill, Barry. *Imagineering an American Dreamscape: Genesis, Evolution, and Redemption of the Regional Theme Park*. Cary, IL: Rivershore Creative, 2020.

Holt, Kermit. "First Color Photo of Disney's 'Mr. Lincoln.'" *Chicago Tribune*, July 31, 1966.

Hobbs, Priscilla. *Walt's Utopia: Disneyland and American Mythmaking*. Jefferson, NC: McFarland & Company, Inc., Publishers, 2015.

Johnson, David. "Disney World as Structure and Symbol: Re-Creation of the American Experience." *The Journal of Popular Culture*, Vol. 15, Issue 1 (Summer 1981): 157–165.

Kennedy, John F. "The New Frontier." Acceptance speech of Senator John F. Kennedy, Democratic National Convention, 15 July 1960. John F. Kennedy Presidential Library and Museum, Boston, MA. Digitized at https://www.jfklibrary.org/asset-viewer/archives/JFKSEN/0910/JFKSEN-0910-015

Kern, Kevin, Tim O'Day and Steven Vagnini. *A Portrait of Walt Disney World: 50 Years of the Most Magical Place on Earth*. Los Angeles: Disney Editions, 2021.

Korkis, Jim. "WDW Chronicles: The Music of Main Street, U.S.A." *All Ears*, March 19, 2013. https://allears.net/wdw-chronicles-the-music-of-main-street-u-s-a

Korkis, Jim. "WDW Chronicles: Year One-Liberty Square 1971." *All Ears*, September 20, 2011. https://allears.net/wdw-chronicles-year-one-liberty-square-1971/

Levin, Amy K., ed. *Defining Memory: Local Museums and the Construction of History in America's Changing Communities*. Lanham, MD: AltaMira Press, 2007.

MacQuarrie, Brian. "Liberty Tree Protest 250 Years Ago Is Marked." *Boston Globe*, August 14, 2015. https://www.bostonglobe.com/metro/2015/08/14/the-liberty-tree-long-gone-and-mostly-forgotten-marks-birthday/pFEXczClYeC4TIKlYdIiEK/story.html

Magic Candle Company. "Space Coaster" candle description. Accessed February 7, 2022. https://magiccandlecompany.com/collections/frontpage/products/space-coaster?ref=popsugar.com

Marling, Karal Ann. "Disneyland, 1955: Just Take the Santa Ana Freeway to the American Dream." *American Art*, Vol. 5, no. ½ (Winter-Spring 1991): 169–207. 10.1086/424113

McDaniel, Brian. *Walt Disney World: The Full Report*. Bloomington, IN: iUniverse, 2008.

Mittermeyer, Sabrina. *A Cultural History of the Disneyland Theme Parks: Middle Class Kingdoms*. Chicago: Intellect Books, 2021.

Nat, Claire. "Magic Kingdom AtMousePhere: The Music of Liberty Square," *Touring Plans*, August 16, 2014, https://touringplans.com/blog/magic-kingdom-atmousephere-music-liberty-square/

Nat, Claire. "Magic Kingdom AtMousePhere: Tomorrowland Music," *Touring Plans Blog*, July 21, 2014, https://touringplans.com/blog/magic-kingdom-tomorrowland-music/

National Science Teacher's Association, "Emotion and Scent," *The Science Teacher*, Vol. 75, No. 9 (December 2008): 18.

Pool, Bob. "Lincoln Liberated," *Los Angeles Times*, August 24, 1990.

Rabinowitz, Richard. *Curating America: Journeys Through Storyscapes of the American Past*. Chapel Hill, NC: The University of North Carolina Press, 2016.

"Science of Disney: Smellitizers." *ThePhDPrincess*. Accessed January 31, 2022. https://phdprincess.com/blog/disney-smells

Silverman, Stephen M. *The Amusement Park: 900 Years of Thrills and Spills, and the Dreamers and Schemers Who Built Them*. New York: Black Dog & Leventhal Publishers, 2019.

Smothers, Marcy Carriker. *Walt's Disneyland: A Walk in the Park with Walt Disney*. Los Angeles: Disney Editions, 2021.

Taylor, Blake. "Extraordinary Magic in Everyday Life," *WDWRadio*, May 1, 2013. https://www.wdwradio.com/2013/05/finding-disney-hidden-disney-smells/

Trickey, Erick, "The Story Behind a Forgotten Symbol of the American Revolution: The Liberty Tree," *Smithsonian Magazine*, May 19, 2016, https://www.smithsonianmag.com/history/story-behind-forgotten-symbol-american-revolution-liberty-tree-180959162/

"The Music of Liberty Square, 1980-Now," *Passport to Dreams*, January 22, 2018, http://passport2dreams.blogspot.com/2016/05/the-music-of-liberty-square-1980-now.html

"The'Sunnyside' of Sleepy Hollow," *Disney Parks Blog*, July 8, 2010, https://disneyparks.disney.go.com/blog/2010/07/the-sunnyside-of-sleepy-hollow/

"Walt and the King of the Wild Frontier." *The Walt Disney Family Museum*, August 17, 2011. https://www.waltdisney.org/blog/walt-and-king-wild-frontier

Wittko, Darren. "Walt Disney World Behind the Magic: Smellitzer Machines," *OrlandoParksGuy.com*, April 27, 2020. https://orlandoparksguy.com/blog/2020/4/26/walt-disney-world-behind-the-magic-smellitzer-machines

Watts, Steven. *The Magic Kingdom: Walt Disney and the American Way of Life*. Columbia, MO: University of Missouri Press, 1997.

4

MICKEY MOUSE/WHITE HOUSE: CELEBRATING AMERICAN IDENTITY AT DISNEY PARKS

As Karal Ann Marling has observed, with its theme parks Disney "added the missing quotient of reality" to the vision of America already being depicted in their cartoons and films. "The once-passive viewer now became ... a real-life participant" in a version of history that seemed more real to those participants than ever before, a version that, to quote David Johnson, became a "special mode of first-hand experience in the repertoire of the great national shared experience."[1] However, it wasn't simply the fact that these memories of America *seemed* real that gave them a place in the national narrative. While the Disney brand identified with American history and values and created a physical space for the formation of collective memories, that was not enough to establish it as a place of *national* memory. What moves the Disney theme parks beyond being just places that create memories of American history into places that create memories of the American national narrative is the legitimization that Disney's parks receive through their partnerships with national figures and celebrations.

One of the most common means of nation-making is the forging of a national narrative to unite the citizenry under one umbrella of identity.[2] Though the federal government preserves and operates "official" sites of American history to tell this narrative, such as National Parks and the Smithsonian Institution, more people are exposed on a regular basis to the "unofficial" Disney version of the national narrative than the federal government's official version. According to the Themed Entertainment Association, in 2016 the Disney theme parks located in the United States received 80.7 million visitors. The National Mall—arguably one of the most important "official" sites for American collective memory, housing numerous National Park Service sites as well as most of the Smithsonian Institution's museums—received 56.5 million visitors in the same year, almost 25 million less than Disney's North American theme parks.[3] For influence, measured by sheer numbers of visitors, Disney almost always comes out on top. Given the Disney

DOI: 10.4324/9781003315094-6

brand's popularity, it isn't surprising that federal and state governments would seek both official and unofficial partnerships with them. In doing so, they appear to accept the Disney version of the American story. Nor is it surprising that Disney would not only welcome but actively seek the promotion potential and implicit seal of approval provided by involving the government and elected officials in events at their parks. This mutually beneficial relationship has served a purpose perhaps not explicitly envisioned by either party: to set Disney's theme parks and the American experience on display there amongst the most important visions of and locations for Americans' collective memory of their national narrative.

Presidents at the Parks

One of the ways the federal government appears to lend its seal of approval to Disney is by literally sending symbolic representatives of the nation to the Disney theme parks themselves. Since Dwight Eisenhower, every president, apart from Lyndon Johnson (who presented Walt Disney with the Medal of Freedom but did not visit his park) and Donald Trump (who was scheduled to visit for a Republican party fundraiser that was canceled), has visited a Disney property at some point in their political lifetime, often for official ceremonies and celebrations.[4] Pre-presidency, Senator John F. Kennedy met with Ahmed Sékou Touré, President of Guinea, at Disneyland while a senator in 1959. Both Richard Nixon and Joe Biden visited when serving as vice president: Nixon visiting Disneyland on August 11, 1955, just a few months after the park's opening, and Biden appearing Disney World's Contemporary Resort in 2011 for a Democratic Party fundraiser. Seven presidents made their visits while in office. Gerald Ford delivered a speech to the National Association of Life Underwriters at the Disneyland Hotel in 1975, and in 1978 Jimmy Carter attended the opening of the 26th World Congress of the International Chamber of Commerce meeting at the Magic Kingdom in Walt Disney World, Florida. Ronald Reagan visited twice, both times to Epcot, part of the Walt Disney World complex, first in 1983 to greet international students there for a fellowship program and then in 1985 to hold a second-term inaugural celebration. George H. W. Bush attended a celebration of his "Points of Light" program at Epcot in 1991, and Bill Clinton spent one night at the now-defunct Disney Institute, a hotel in the Walt Disney World complex, in 1996. George W. Bush stopped at the Grand Floridian hotel at Walt Disney World for a fundraiser in 2003. Barack Obama visited Disney World twice in 2012, first in January when he gave remarks concerning travel to and within the United States while standing in front of Cinderella's Castle and again in June to deliver a speech at the National Association of Latino Elected and Appointed Officials conference. Many presidents have visited after holding office, notably Harry Truman in 1957 and Dwight Eisenhower in 1961.

When sitting presidents visit a Disney Park, in almost every case they declare an explicit connection between Disney Parks and the American experience. When George H.W. Bush celebrated his administration's Points of Light program, which honored community volunteers, at Epcot in 1991, he declared that all had gathered in an "extraordinary place" to "celebrate the American spirit, the greatest natural resource of this, the greatest Nation in the entire world."[5] During his 2012 speech, President Obama explicitly connected Disney and the American Dream, describing America as a place where

> hard work pays off, where responsibility is rewarded, and where anybody can make it if they try. That's part of the reason why people want to come here, because they know our history. They know what the American Dream has been all about ... a place like Disneyland represents that quintessentially American spirit. This image is something that's recognized all around the world.[6]

Not only do presidential visits offer the occasion for great photo-ops and good PR for both the administration and the Disney Company, but they confer the ultimate legitimization of Disney as the seat of collective memory of, as President Obama put it, "that quintessentially American spirit."

The simple fact that almost every president has visited a Disney theme park property sets the parks apart from other themed entertainment offerings as places of importance to the American narrative. However, certain visits warrant further study for the ways in which they had outsize effects on the legitimization of Disney's national narrative.

Richard Nixon Sets the Precedent

Undoubtedly the president who did the most to craft the relationship between Disney Parks and the White House is Richard Nixon. Nixon was born in Yorba Linda, California, just a few miles from the Anaheim orange groves where Walt Disney would later build Disneyland. By the 1950s, Nixon had become a political player in California, and had more than one opportunity to hobnob with Walt and Roy Disney. The families were well enough acquainted that in a 1959 letter Walt Disney addressed the sitting Vice President familiarly, as "Dear Dick Nixon" and referenced that he'd recently been speaking with Nixon's brother, Don, then a California businessman.[7] As a former Senator from California and a life-long California resident, Nixon had a vested interest in Disneyland's success and what it might mean for the state. As Vice President and later as President, he had a responsibility to encourage business which he felt was beneficial to the nation at large. This, plus what seems to have been a genuine enjoyment of the theme parks, may have had a hand in driving his involvement with both Disneyland and Walt Disney World, which set the precedent for Disney theme parks as sites of presidential pilgrimage for administrations to come.

Vice President Nixon brought his wife and two daughters to the newly opened Disneyland on the first official trip by the office of a president on August 11, 1955. The family toured the park, and Nixon clearly enjoyed himself—when he boarded the ride Peter Pan's Flight his wife Pat said, "Dick's getting a bigger kick out of this than the kids!"[8] But beyond merely strolling the streets and posing for photo ops, Nixon took part in a ceremony on the steps of Main Street's City Hall in which he was gifted a "key to Disneyland" from Vice President and General Manager of the park, C. V. Wood Jr. Traditionally a "key to the city" is meant to confer welcome on the bearer, a symbolic gesture representing what was once the giving of a literal key to a medieval city's gates. An Alabama newspaper called the key "an 'open sesame' for the Vice President and his family to the 160 acres of this fairyland come-to-life."[9] The large Yale key, nestled in a lined wooden box and now residing at the Richard Nixon Presidential Library and Museum, was a gesture of welcome not just to Nixon himself, but to the office he represented, that of the President of the United States. It is the ultimate symbol of just how enmeshed the Disneyland version of the American narrative was with the prevailing "official" narrative from the park's very opening, that the representative of that official narrative was offered carte blanche access, even if only symbolically, to the Disneyland grounds.

The Nixon family returned for another public trip in 1959, participating in the official opening of the Disneyland Monorail, Matterhorn Bobsleds and Submarine Voyage. The Second Family cut the ribbon for the Monorail, creating another moment when, as in the presentation of a Disneyland key, the federal government partnered with Walt Disney to welcome the public into Disney's vision of the national narrative. Reporter Joan Winchell made note of how the opening ceremonies, which brought together traditional pomp and circumstance and certified American celebrities, both political and cultural, created a uniquely "American" feeling moment. Winchell found herself seated next to the Nixon family and other "public heroes," and noted:

> A wave of it-could-only-happen-in-America pride assailed us as we watched not only the triumphant [Meredith] Willson (who was counting pennies a few years back), but emcee Art Linkletter (who started life as an orphan but learned early about the power of positive thinking), and the Hero Of The Day, Walt Disney himself, who while reigning over his $23 million wonderland, surely must have thought of the day he arrived in Hollywood in 1923 with only $40 to his name and a pocketful of dreams.[10]

Nixon's successful presidential campaign was even associated with Disneyland, when Nixon stumped down Main Street, U.S.A., on August 16, 1968. Even amongst Disneyland's delights, he was a popular attraction in his own right, and his Secret Service detail was "all but trampled in their efforts to keep the crowds from getting too close."[11] Nixon's many Disneyland visits were largely responsible for the creation of the strong association between the White House and Mickey Mouse, to the point where many presidential hopefuls have visited or been associated with Disney theme parks in the years since. Raymond Coffey reported in 1976 that while at Disneyland

Jimmy Carter was shaking hands with Mickey Mouse. Somehow ABC-TV hadn't set up its camera in time and missed the picture. Correspondent Sam Donaldson was steaming.

"Dammit," the aggrieved Donaldson explained to Carter's media managers. "When a candidate for President shakes hands with Mickey Mouse that's news."[12]

The story is apocryphal, as no evidence of it exists in other sources, but it is illustrative of the level to which Mickey Mouse and Disneyland had become associated with the highest office in the land. As a journalist noted when Vice President George H. W. Bush kicked off his own 1988 presidential campaign at Disneyland, "They're not exactly the White House, 'Hail to the Chief' and the American eagle. But Disneyland, 'Zip-A-Dee-Doo-Dah' and Mickey Mouse work just fine when you're running for president and want to be associated with national symbols."[13]

As Nixon had conferred a sense of federal approval on Disneyland at its opening as the Vice President, he also had occasion to do so for Walt Disney World, as he was the sitting President when it opened in 1971. As opening ceremonies for Disney World were coming together, the President was planning to attend. By early October, Nixon and his Chief of Staff, H.R. Haldeman, were planning for a quick visit where, Haldeman told the President,

> You'd go around ... They also have this Hall of Presidents which has an interesting twist 'cause they have living figures of all of the presidents, each one of 'em talks or something, including you, which is a little awkward.[14]

Plans started coming together for the trip, with Nixon and Haldeman discussing the possibility of giving an official White House flag to the theme park as a token of support.

Nixon: The more I think about it the more I think the Disneyland thing is perhaps worth it.

...

Haldeman: You don't have to do it, or you can do it on the way down Friday.

Nixon: Just stop down and give 'em a flag?

Haldeman: Sure.

Nixon: Make that the news.

Haldeman: And that's the weekend before their grand opening week, that's the date, their grand opening starts on Saturday.

Nixon: And I'd go in the day before.

Haldeman: So, you'd go in the day before which would be great for them, set them up.

Nixon: Go ahead and give 'em—that would be enjoyable too

Haldeman:	Give 'em a flag—
Nixon:	Go around and see all the rides, and the presidents' thing, we bring 'em a flag and so forth. Check that out, will you?
	…
Nixon:	Disneyland on the way down would be really great.
	…
Nixon:	But the Disney thing is gonna be interesting thing to do. To do it would be interesting. Be a hell of a good time.[15]

By mid-October, the rumor had gotten out in central Florida that the President was coming for Walt Disney World's grand opening. In fact, security preparations had begun as of October 15.[16] However, private conversations revealed via the Nixon White House tapes make it clear that there was doubt as to the appropriateness at that time of a visit to the new "Vacation Kingdom of the World." The administration was planning to announce troop reductions and the cessation of offensives in Vietnam, and Nixon was concerned that a visit to a vacation destination would seem callous as the public awaited the Vietnam announcements.

Nixon:	On the Disneyland thing. I'm inclined to think that we'd better not do it, I'll tell you why. Henry's[17] getting back on the 25th and ah, we've got that troop announcement coming up shortly thereafter. You see what I mean?
	…
Nixon:	I'm inclined to think that Camp David is nice and upright, you know what I mean, and it's one of those times, it's very pleasant, I don't mind going out there, well, I don't mind any time but … Well, what I'm getting at is hold Disneyland in terms of that. I think I should be here. Because when he comes back then I will have to consider, what the whole impression will be. I can't do a press event until I'm ready to go on the troop announcement, see?
	…
Nixon:	Well, get a flag down there at least.
Haldeman:	We can take care of that.
Nixon:	I think we can say that. Say that I send a flag from the White House. Disneyland after he gets back. Because I want to be here when he gets back. I want to be here right away when he gets back.[18]

The resolution was for Nixon to send H.R. Haldeman and Press Secretary Ronald Ziegler, a former Jungle Cruise skipper at Disneyland, as his administration's representatives for the ceremonial Walt Disney World opening. Haldeman presented Roy O. Disney with a flag that had flown over the White House, emphasizing that it was "the first Mr. Nixon ha[d] personally sent out to anyone."[19] Accompanying the flag was a letter from the President that emphasized the park's importance to American identity:

This letter brings with it my heartiest congratulations and warmest greetings to you and all of those who have worked so successfully to make Walt Disney World an enchanting reality. Your kingdom of fantasy will entertain and delight millions from all ages, from all lands, and in this spirit of goodwill, I take special pleasure in presenting you with the flag of the United States which was flown over the White House. As it is raised in Town Square, may it represent our faith in the American dream which is so much in evidence at Walt Disney World. May this flag further serve as a symbol of hope to your visitors from around the world and give cause for mutual understanding.[20]

The flag was reportedly flying "briskly over Main Street, U.S.A., as final dedication ceremonies were completed and the last roll of film was shot for an NBC national television spectacular."[21] As Disneyland had welcomed the White House with the symbolic gift of a key to Vice President Nixon, so Nixon symbolically welcomed Walt Disney World into the pantheon of American pilgrimage locations by anointing it with a White House flag.

While Nixon was in the White House, he set one more precedent in the White House–Disney Park relationship. On November 17, 1973, the President participated in a question-and-answer session for the Annual Convention of Associated Press Managing Editors, held at the Contemporary Hotel at the Walt Disney World Resort. The quick stop would have been notable mostly by historians of Disney for being the first of its type, a sitting president in a sense "blessing" a Disney theme park with their presence, had Nixon not made one of the most infamous statements of his entire presidency just steps from the gates of the Magic Kingdom.

At the time of Nixon's Disney World visit, his presidency was mired in the Watergate Scandal, including an investigation into the suspicions that Nixon had been complicit in illegal affairs done on behalf of his presidential campaign, and that he had unduly profited from his time in public service. As Nixon fielded questions from the 400 reporters at the Disney World press conference, the scandal was front and center, causing Nixon to declare, "I have earned every cent. And in all of my years of public life, I have never obstructed justice. People have got to know whether or not their president is a crook. Well, I'm not a crook. I've earned everything I've got."[22] The line, "I am not a crook" quickly became a defining one of Nixon's presidency, particularly after the scandals ultimately resulted in his resignation.[23] As a result, Walt Disney World became not just a place where presidents visited, or conducted business, but also a place where they made lasting history.

Subsequent presidents continued this relationship by making official appearances on Disney Park grounds. Gerald Ford gave a televised address from the Disneyland Hotel in September 1975, and Jimmy Carter opening the 26th International Chamber of Commerce from the Cinderella Castle stage in Disney World.[24] While Disney Parks were firmly established as locations for official presidential business by the time of his presidency, Ronald Reagan's 1985 visit took this relationship a step further, using Disney World as a ceremonial space akin to Washington, D.C.

Ronald Reagan's Disney Legacy

Before assuming office, Ronald Reagan had a relationship with Disneyland stemming from his days as a Hollywood actor when he served as co-host of the live *Dateline Disneyland* special that showcased the opening day of Disneyland in 1955. While as a California resident and member of the entertainment business Reagan had been invested in the cultural and economic success of the theme park since its opening, in 1967 he was elected governor of California, giving him political investment in Disneyland's success as well. During his first term as president, Reagan visited Epcot to speak to a group of students participating in the President's International Youth Exchange initiative via Walt Disney World's World Showcase Fellowship Program.[25]

As Reagan's second term began in January 1985, frigid temperatures settled over Washington, D.C., canceling all planned outdoor celebrations, including the inaugural parade. To fill the ceremonial gap, Disney offered to host a spring festival of the high school marching band, which could function as a mini-inaugural parade. Paid for by Disney and other private corporations, 2,700 students were brought to Florida to perform at Epcot Center on Memorial Day.[26] After the traditional wreath-laying at Arlington National Cemetery that morning, Reagan flew to Orlando to watch his belated inaugural celebrations. He used his platform at Epcot to announce that he intended to soon outline a tax proposal that, in his words, would "launch a new American revolution."[27] Reagan's new American revolution was announced from Disney's vision of our colonial collective memory, the American Adventure.

The impact of this event was threefold. First, holding an administration-sanctioned event to celebrate an inauguration, one that in fact replaced the original inaugural event planned for the traditional ceremonial space in Washington, D.C., affirmed physical Disney Park spaces as locations for official, uniquely American moments, in this case, the peaceful transition of power that defines American democracy. Second, the event was held on Memorial Day, an American holiday dedicated to remembering U.S. military personnel who have died in the course of duty. The presence of the president at Walt Disney World on such a hallowed American holiday marked Disney as an acceptable place for all Americans to observe that holiday. Third, Reagan's use of a Disney theme park to publicly announce a "new American revolution" symbolically placed Disney's American Adventure alongside the locations that are today part of our collective memory of the American Revolution, such as Independence Hall in Philadelphia or the Old State House in Boston. While the architecture and content of the American Adventure were inspired by the actual locations where Revolutionary activities took place, the Disney pavilion is merely a copy, meant to evoke memories of that history. That is, it was, until a president used it as a place from which to mark his own version of an American revolution.

National Celebrations

Another way the Disney theme parks have earned a sense of legitimization from the state is through the staging of national moments of celebration and the use of American symbols. In addition to the inaugural parade for Reagan, these celebrations have included yearly Fourth of July celebrations and daily flag retreat ceremonies. Mickey Mouse and company had become symbols of America outside of the company during World War II. Now, the prominent presence of American symbols, particularly the American flag, within the Disney Parks themselves reinforced their integration as places telling versions of the official national story.

In 1991 an entertainment analyst noted, "if you had to identify one company most closely associated with the American flag, it would have to be Disney."[28] For decades, Disney Parks have celebrated the quintessentially American holiday of July 4th with fireworks, parades, and a plethora of merchandise featuring both Mickey Mouse and the American flag. These celebrations have often been recorded and broadcast for the greater public and, in the age of social media, livestreamed to create a real-time shared experience connecting Disney spaces with America's birthday for those there physically and those thousands of miles away. A 1974 newspaper article ran a photograph they captioned "The world of Disney—including the American flag and Cinderella's Castle," not just equating the American flag with Disney but almost subsuming it into the Disney universe, of equal status with their iconic castle.[29]

Disney Parks have flown the American flag over Town Square, the symbolic heart of the American narrative at Disney, since Disneyland's opening in 1955. Reporter Charles Mercer felt that the opening day ceremony, as captured on the special *Dateline: Disneyland*, in fact, focused *too* much on the initial flag-raising ceremony. "One's patriotism should not be questioned when he wonders about the interest in the elaborate flag-raising ceremonies at Disneyland. It is not, after all, a national shrine."[30] The focus on the elaborate flag raising, which was repeated with the flag sent by President Nixon to Walt Disney World in 1971, served to set the stage for the ongoing strong association between the American flag and the Disney Parks.

While the flag raisings at the opening of the parks were publicized events that showed the world that Disney Parks were committed to their patriotic place as part of the United States, it is daily flag retreat ceremonies held on both coasts since those first ceremonial openings that consistently reinforce the Disney Parks as distinctly American spaces. The exact ceremony particulars have varied over time, but they have generally involved Disney Security cast members performing the lowering, some recognition of veterans at the park, and often music, either piped in or live from various cast performers. While many public spaces in the United States fly an American flag daily and observe U.S. flag codes with regards to raising and lowering them, few places outside of military bases regularly observe a full ceremonial flag lowering. For many Disney Parks visitors, the ceremony on Main Street, U.S.A., may be the only flag retreat they have ever observed or participated in, making it a distinctly American ceremony that, for those visitors, is forever tied to Disney. In Disneyland's 25th year, a cast member magazine noted the importance of the event, especially when contrasted against the world outside Disney gates: "In a day when patriotism is considered a lost art, this simple ceremony has a magical quality that can stir the most cynical soul." The magazine went on to ask cast members to be sure that when on duty they "remember to observe the ceremony with proper respect" to telegraph to guests the "appreciation for our own country … celebrated each day on Main Street."[31]

Disneyland and Walt Disney World were both closed for over three months in 2020 due to the Covid-19 pandemic. During that time, then-president of Walt Disney World Resort, Josh D'Amaro, posted a video on his Instagram account showing that Disney security cast members were continuing to raise and lower the flag even during the park's closure. He captioned it:

> While our world looks very different today, one thing endures … the American flag still flies over Walt Disney World. I'm inspired how our Security Cast Members continue to raise it each and every morning at Magic Kingdom while they are on duty protecting the magic. It's a symbol that we're still here and will not falter.[32]

Tellingly, D'Amaro doesn't make clear whether the "unfaltering we" he refers to is Walt Disney World or the nation itself. Whether he intended to or not, D'Amaro equates the symbol of the American flag and Walt Disney World itself with America as a united nation that is "still here" and "will not falter." Disneyland, too, continued to lower the flag during its pandemic closure. Upon reopening, cast member and Navy veteran Nick Filippone commented, "we have been honored to continue Walt's patriotic legacy with keeping the American flag flying throughout the park's closure showing that no matter what else was happening, we could maintain this element of our heritage."[33] Again, it is unclear whether Filippone is referring to Disneyland's heritage or America's heritage. This is exactly what the strong association between the two symbols has helped to craft: a blurring between "Disney" and "America."

These regular patriotic events provide a steady drumbeat of patriotism and a reminder of Disney Parks' place in our collective identity formation, and they serve to continually reinforce the parks' status as quasi-official national narrative repositories. In addition to these regular events, two major historical moments for Disney and the United States explicitly connected Disney Park spaces to national patriotic celebrations.

America on Parade

Of all the patriotic celebrations held at Disney theme parks over the last 60 years, perhaps the largest was the 15-month bicoastal extravaganza of Americana, "America on Parade," which Disney staged from 1975 to 1976 to celebrate the bicentennial of the United States.

FIGURE 4.1   Disney's version of *The Spirit of '76*.

Source: Courtesy of Diana "Dede" Johnson, former Walt Disney World Zoo Crew Cast Member.

At the head of the 50-float parade was the Disneyfied version of *The Spirit of '76*, a famous painting by Archibald Willard made to celebrate the 100th anniversary of the American Revolution in 1876. While the historic painting features an unnamed flag bearer, drummer boy, and fifer in the Revolutionary army as they march into battle, Disney's float featured Mickey Mouse, Goofy and Donald Duck as the bearer, drummer, and fifer, respectively. "The People of America," 150 cast members dressed as 8–10 foot tall historically inspired characters, marched alongside or stood atop floats meant to depict important moments and ideals from American history. The choices of historic moments and myths are reflective of the national narrative at the time-largely white and focused on technological progress and innovation. Featured vignettes included Betsy Ross' (mythic) sewing of the American flag, the completion of the Transcontinental Railroad and various celebrations of technology and progress on floats depicting transportation. Individual states were celebrated weekly according to the order in which they were admitted to the Union.[34] Notably absent (as was true in many civic celebrations of this time) were vignettes that centered people of color as actors in these identity-forming historic moments.

Designated as official bicentennial events by the U.S. Government and taking place at both Disneyland and Walt Disney World, these parades ran twice a day on two coasts for over a year and were estimated to have been seen by over 25 million people.[35] Independence National Historic Park, the seat of the actual signing of the Declaration of Independence which the year's celebrations marked, received by contrast 3.7 million visitors in 1976.[36] The sheer numbers witnessing Disney's parade made it one of the largest shared bicentennial celebrations in the nation. This sense of national celebration taking place specifically at Disney sites did much to solidify the theme park's place in the minds of Americans as spaces not only for family-friendly vacations but as ones where they could come together to share cultural and historical heritage. After visiting both the Magic Kingdom at Walt Disney World in Florida and Colonial Williamsburg during the bicentennial celebrations, journalist Dick Schaap's six-year-old son intimated to his father, "George Washington may be the father of this country, dad, but Walt Disney is its guardian." Schaap himself astutely (and wryly) observed how the celebration placed the Disney theme parks alongside another living history park as a repository of national heritage and place of celebration.

> The cradle of democracy blends with the height of imagination, and every day through September, 1976, 'America on Parade,' a spectacular Bicentennial salute, marches straight down ... not Duke of Gloucester Street in Williamsburg ... but Main Street, U.S.A., in the heart of Disney World. And there, at the heart of the parade, bearing drum and fife and Betsy Ross's original pennant, dressed in tricorner hat and patched with bandages, stand the three symbols of the American Revolution: Mickey Mouse, Donald Duck, and Goofy.[37]

Ten years later, Walt Disney World again took part in a bicentennial celebration of the American government, this time the 200th anniversary of the U.S. Constitution. Festivities included a display of original Constitution-related artifacts at Epcot, which exhibited a desk used by James Madison to draft parts of the central document, special fireworks and shows, and a Constitution-themed parade, the "We the People All America Parade," which featured Mickey and Minnie in colonial dress riding atop a very large copy of the document. Disney promotional materials touted the events as "America's biggest and best Bicentennial party" that was sure to "bring out the red, white & blue in you!"[38] Once again, Disney's festivities were sanctioned by the official national commission, headed by retired Chief Justice of the Supreme Court Warren Burger. The commission stated that its goal for the bicentennial was more education than outright celebration; spokesman for the commission Chuck Timanus said they were aiming for a "cerebral celebration."[39] It was surprising to some, then, when Burger chose to kick off the festivities not from somewhere like

Philadelphia, where the Constitutional Convention of 1787 took place, but at Walt Disney World.[40]

To Burger, however, the pairing of the commission and Disney were ideal. "Disney is a patriotic, history-minded enterprise," he said as he presented Walt Disney World with the loan of artifacts for the Epcot exhibition. Senator Ted Kennedy noted at the event that "This has not lessened or cheapened the importance of the Constitution because we need to insure that as many people as possible read it," implying that Disney World was one of the best locations from which to reach a majority of America.[41] Then-chairman and chief executive officer of Walt Disney Co. Michael Eisner said, "No company is better able to communicate with the American public than the Disney company."[42] Burger further stressed that the Constitution, after all, belonged not to "lawyers and judges. It belongs to everybody, and we hope that will be the kind of celebration we'll have."[43] While the celebration legitimized Disney Parks as places for official celebration, it also suggested that Disney was a place where the narrative and identity celebrated was one that belonged not only to the federal government but to the American people.

The three-day "media bash" that kicked off the constitutional celebration wasn't solely to celebrate the birth of America's governance, however. Held in the first week of October 1986, it was a joint celebration of the U.S. Constitution's anniversary, and Walt Disney World's 15th birthday year. When Burger spoke on the Constitution, it was in front of a "30-foot logo of Disney World's anniversary."[44] Not only did the event continue to stress Disney Parks as places for official representation and celebration of American national identity, tying the national celebration of one of the country's foundational documents to the birthday of Walt Disney World naturally elevated the resort's own existence and celebration as a moment of national importance.

Partnerships with the federal government during World War II had already given the Disney brand some sense of authority in representing the United States. With the opening of Disneyland, Disney continued to invite and/or accept politicians at their parks, drawing, perhaps unconsciously, on the legitimacy of the state in the process of nation-making and creating a national story to burnish their own authority in those activities. Patriotism was always a foundational principle in Disney Park spaces. However, it was and is the continued validation the parks receive through visits from governmental figures and official national celebrations that place the Disney Parks alongside sites such as the National Mall and the White House ellipse, and Independence Hall as American ceremonial spaces.

Notes

1 David Johnson quoted in Stephen Fjellman, *Vinyl Leaves: Walt Disney World and America* (Boulder, CO: Westview Press, 1992), 96.
2 See John Gillis, ed. *Commemorations: The Politics of National Identity* (Princeton: Princeton University Press, 1994) for a discussion of the politics of national identity and collective memory.

3 "Theme Index Museum Index 2016 Global Attractions Attendance Report," *Themed Entertainment Association*, accessed May 5, 2018. http://www.teaconnect.org/images/ files/TEA_235_103719_170601.pdf. "2016 Visitor Statistics Washington, DC," *Destination DC*, accessed May 5, 2018. https://washington-org.s3.amazonaws.com/ s3fs-public/2016_visitor_statistics_september_2017.pdf.

4 Steven Lemongello, "Trump's a No-Go for Orlando as Florida GOP Dinner Moves to Miami instead," *Orlando Sentinel*, November 19, 2019, https://www.orlandosentinel.com/ politics/os-ne-trump-florida-gop-20191119-yqzgrh5ubjb5nl7fcdy3a3pl5q-story.html.

5 James Gerstenzang, "Bush, Mickey Mouse Praise Points of Light Program," *Los Angeles Times*, October 1, 1990, OCA18 and George H.W. Bush, "Remarks at the Daily Points of Light Celebration in Orlando, Florida," *George H.W. Bush Presidential Library and Museum*, https://bush41library.tamu.edu/archives/public-papers/3441.

6 Obama, "Remarks at Walt Disney World."

7 Letter, Walt Disney to Richard Nixon, Folder 6/14/1959 Disneyland-California Trip, Box 108, Series 207, Richard Nixon Pre-Presidential Materials, Richard Nixon Presidential Library and Museum, Yorba Linda, California.

8 "Nixon Takes Time Out for Disneyland: Vice President and Family Prove to be Top Attractions," *Los Angeles Times*, August 12, 1955, 2.

9 "Wonderland Doors Open for Nixons," *The Choctaw Advocate*, February 9, 1956.

10 Joan Winchell, "Disneyland, Revisited," *Los Angeles Times*, June 16, 1959, A1.

11 "Police Coordinate Protection for Nixon at Rally in Anaheim," *Los Angeles Times*, September 15, 1968, OC1.

12 Raymond Coffey, "TV Makes Politics a Trivia Game," *Chicago Tribune*, November 9, 1980, A6.
    There is no evidence that Jimmy Carter visited Disneyland in 1976, but he may have met Mickey Mouse at other events, notably a press conference held at the Anaheim Convention Center close to Disneyland in 1975, or when he was greeted by a child dressed as Mickey Mouse on the campaign trail in Columbus, Ohio, in 1976.

13 Mitchell Locin, "Candidates Seek Right Setting," *Chicago Tribune*, September 6, 1988, 1.

14 OVAL 576-11, September 20, 1971, Nixon White House Tapes; Richard Nixon Presidential Library and Museum, Yorba Linda, California, accessed via nixontapes.org.

15 OVAL 584-3, October 5, 1971, Nixon White House Tapes. Note that Nixon seems often to refer to Disneyland when he means Walt Disney World, likely due to his familiarity with the original park.

16 "Nixon to Visit Orlando," *Orlando Sentinel*, October 15, 1971, 31.

17 Henry Kissinger, Secretary of State and National Security Advisor.

18 OVAL 594-2, October 18, 1971, Nixon White House Tapes.

19 Jean Yothers, "30,000 See Wonders of Opening Day," *Orlando Sentinel*, October 25, 1971, 1.

20 Letter, Richard Nixon to Roy Disney, Folder Disney, Box 18, White House Central Files, Richard Nixon Presidential Library and Museum, Yorba Linda, California.

21 "Dedication Hails Man's Imagination," *Orlando Evening Star*, October 27, 1971, 39.

22 Carroll Kilpatrick, "Nixon Tells Editors, 'I'm Not a Crook," *The Washington Post*, November 18, 1973, A1.

23 A 1995 survey of 2,000 Americans found that 100% recognized the line. "Nixon's 'Crook' Line Is Most Recognized," *Chicago Defender*, January 18, 1995, 15.

24 President's Daily Diary, September 21, 1975, Box 77, Gerald R. Ford Presidential Library and Museum, Grand Rapids, Michigan, and President's Daily Diary, October 1, 1978, The Jimmy Carter Presidential Library and Museum, Atlanta, Georgia, available online at https://www.jimmycarterlibrary.gov/assets/documents/diary/1978/d100178t.pdf.

25 Presidential Briefing Papers, March 8, 1983, Office of the President, Presidential Briefing Papers: Records, 1981–1989, Case File 127508, Box 27, Ronald Reagan Presidential Foundation and Institute, Simi Valley, California, available digitally at

https://www.reaganlibrary.gov/sites/default/files/digitallibrary/smof/president/presidentialbriefingpapers/box-027/40–439-5730647-027-006–2016.pdf.

26 "Bands Slated for Inaugural Finally to Play for Reagan," *The Hartford Courant*, May 27, 1985, A2C.

27 Ronald Reagan, "Remarks to Participants in the President's Inaugural Bands Parade at Walt Disney's EPCOT Center Near Orlando, Florida," May 27, 1985, Ronald Reagan Presidential Foundation and Institute, available at https://www.reaganlibrary.gov/research/speeches/52785a.

28 Paul C. Marsh quoted in Chris Woodyard, "Disneyland Offers Returning Troops 2 Free Tickets Each," *Los Angeles Times*, March 9, 1991.

29 "Fish Eye View of Tomorrow," *The Orlando Sentinel*, February 3, 1974, 117.

30 Mercer can be forgiven for misunderstanding Disney's place in the American narrative, as it had only just opened (scholars today refer to it as a national shrine all the time). Charles Mercer, "'Disneyland' Is Dedicated in Confusion," *Wellsville Daily Reporter*, Wellsville, NY, July 21, 1955, 8.

31 "A Patriotic Retreat," *Disneyland Line*, Vol. 12, no. 11, March 13, 1980, Political and Military History Collections, National Museum of American History, Smithsonian Institution.

32 Josh D'Amaro, Video of Walt Disney World flag raising, *Instagram video*, April 1, 2020, https://www.instagram.com/p/B-cNXSwjnDO/.

33 Brittani Tuttle, "Flag Retreat Ceremonies Return to Walt Disney World, Disneyland," *Attractions Magazine*, July 5, 2021, https://attractionsmagazine.com/flag-retreat-ceremonies-return-walt-disney-world-disneyland/.

34 Edgar and Patricia Cheatham, "Disney's salute to the Bicentennial," *Chicago Tribune*, September 28, 1975, 4.

35 James T. Wooten, "Disney Will Join in Bicentennial," *New York Times,* February 19, 1975.

36 "Independence NHP," National Park Service, accessed May 21, 2018. https://irma.nps.gov/Stats/SSRSReports/Park%20Specific%20Reports/Annual%20Park%20Recreation%20Visitation%20(1904%20-%20Last%20Calendar%20Year)?Park=INDE.

37 Dick Schaap, "Culture Shock," *New York Times,* September 28, 1975.

38 "We the People" promotional flier, Political and Military History Collections, National Museum of American History, Smithsonian Institution.

39 "Constitution's Bicentennial," *United Press International*, January 25, 1987, https://www.upi.com/Archives/1987/01/25/Constitutions-bicentennialNEWLNWe-the-People-celebrateConstitutions-200th-anniversary/3594538549200/.

40 Both Burger and Disney World took some criticism for partnering in what some called "hyping history" and, for Burger, "shedding judicial dignity." "Constitution's Bicentennial," Joan Chrissos, "How Far Will They Go," *The Miami Herald*, October 20, 1986, 56, and Aaron Epstein, "Retired Chief Justice Defends His Record," *The Miami Herald*, December 14, 1986, 10A.

41 He had a point. A poll conducted at Epcot during the celebration showed that 60% of Disney guests did not know the phrase "We the People" came from the Constitution. "'We the People' don't know," *Sapulpa Daily Herald* [Sapulpa, OK], September 16, 1987, 3B. Kennedy quoted in Craig Crawford, "Kennedy: Popularizing the Constitution Isn't Commercializing It," *The Orlando Sentinel*, October 5, 1986, https://www.orlandosentinel.com/news/os-xpm-1986-10-05–0260110062-story.html.

42 Ron Word, "Burger, Daniloff at Constitution Fete at Disney World," *Associated Press*, October 4, 1986, https://apnews.com/article/47e9c20ccfab6f07cfcb26d5e3ce2419.

43 "Burger Considers Putting Constitution into Markets," *Times-Advocate* [Escondido, CA], October 5, 1986, B4.

44 Craig Crawford, "Burger Whips Up Constitution Fervor," *The Orlando Sentinel*, October 4, 1986, A6.

References

"2016 Visitor Statistics Washington, DC." *Destination DC.* Accessed May 5, 2018. https://washington-org.s3.amazonaws.com/s3fs-public/2016_visitor_statistics_september_2017.pdf

"A Patriotic Retreat." *Disneyland Line*, Vol. 12, no. 11 (March 13, 1980). Political and Military History Collections, National Museum of American History, Smithsonian Institution.

"Bands Slated for Inaugural Finally to Play for Reagan." *The Hartford Courant*, May 27, 1985.

"Burger Considers Putting Constitution into Markets." *Times-Advocate* [Escondido, CA], October 5, 1986.

Bush, George H.W. "Remarks at the Daily Points of Light Celebration in Orlando, Florida." George H.W. Bush Presidential Library and Museum. https://bush41library.tamu.edu/archives/public-papers/3441

Cheatham, Edgar and Patricia. "Disney's salute to the Bicentennial." *Chicago Tribune*, September 28, 1975.

Chrissos, Joan. "How Far Will They Go," *The Miami Herald*, October 20, 1986.

Crawford, Craig. "Burger Whips Up Constitution Fervor." *The Orlando Sentinel*, October 4, 1986.

Crawford, Craig. "Kennedy: Popularizing the Constitution Isn't Commercializing It." *The Orlando Sentinel*, October 5, 1986, https://www.orlandosentinel.com/news/os-xpm-1986-10-05-0260110062-story.html

Coffey, Raymond. "TV Makes Politics a Trivia Game." *Chicago Tribune*, November 9, 1980.

"Constitution's Bicentennial." *United Press International*, January 25, 1987. https://www.upi.com/Archives/1987/01/25/Constitutions-bicentennialNEWLNWe-the-People-celebrateConstitutions-200th-anniversary/3594538549200/

D'Amaro, Josh. "Video of Walt Disney World flag raising" *Instagram video*, April 1, 2020. https://www.instagram.com/p/B-cNXSwjnDO/

"Dedication Hails Man's Imagination." *Orlando Evening Star*, October 27, 1971.

Epstein, Aaron. "Retired Chief Justice Defends His Record." *The Miami Herald*, December 14, 1986.

"Fish Eye View of Tomorrow." *The Orlando Sentinel*, February 3, 1974.

Fjellman, Stephen. *Vinyl Leaves: Walt Disney World and America.* Boulder, CO: Westview Press, 1992.

Gerstenzang, James. "Bush, Mickey Mouse Praise Points of Light Program." *Los Angeles Times*, October 1, 1990.

Gillis, John, ed. *Commemorations: The Politics of National Identity.* Princeton, NJ: Princeton University Press, 1994.

"Independence NHP." National Park Service. Accessed May 21, 2018. https://irma.nps.gov/Stats/SSRSReports/Park%20Specific%20Reports/Annual%20Park%20Recreation%20Visitation%20(1904%20-%20Last%20Calendar%20Year)?Park=INDE

Kilpatrick, Carroll. "Nixon Tells Editors, 'I'm Not a Crook." *The Washington Post*, November 18, 1973.

Lemongello, Steven. "Trump's a no-go for Orlando as Florida GOP dinner moves to Miami instead." *Orlando Sentinel*, November 19, 2019. https://www.orlandosentinel.com/politics/os-ne-trump-florida-gop-20191119-yqzgrh5ubjb5nl7fcdy3a3pl5q-story.html

Locin, Mitchell. "Candidates Seek Right Setting." *Chicago Tribune*, September 6, 1988.

Mercer, Charles. "Disneyland' Is Dedicated in Confusion." *Wellsville Daily Reporter*, Wellsville, NY, July 21, 1955.

"Nixon Takes Time Out for Disneyland: Vice President and Family Prove to be Top Attractions." *Los Angeles Times*, August 12, 1955.

"Nixon to Visit Orlando." *Orlando Sentinel,* October 15, 1971.

"Nixon's 'Crook' Line Is Most Recognized." *Chicago Defender,* January 18, 1995.

Nixon White House Tapes. Richard Nixon Presidential Library and Museum. Yorba Linda, California. Accessed via nixontapes.org

Obama, Barack. "Remarks at Walt Disney World in Lake Buena Vista, Florida." The White House, January 19, 2012. https://obamawhitehouse.archives.gov/the-press-office/2012/01/19/remarks-president-unveiling-strategy-help-boost-travel-and-tourism

Office of the President, Presidential Briefing Papers. Ronald Reagan Presidential Foundation and Institute. Simi Valley, California. Available digitally at https://www.reaganlibrary.gov/sites/default/files/digitallibrary/smof/president/presidentialbriefing-papers/box-027/40–439-5730647-027-006–2016.pdf

"Police Coordinate Protection for Nixon at Rally in Anaheim." *Los Angeles Times,* September 15, 1968.

President's Daily Diary. *Gerald R. Ford Presidential Library and Museum.* Grand Rapids, Michigan.

President's Daily Diary. *The Jimmy Carter Presidential Library and Museum.* Atlanta, Georgia. Available online at https://www.jimmycarterlibrary.gov/assets/documents/diary/1978/d100178t.pdf

Reagan, Ronald. "Remarks to Participants in the President's Inaugural Bands Parade at Walt Disney's EPCOT Center Near Orlando, Florida." May 27, 1985. Ronald Reagan Presidential Foundation and Institute. Simi Valley, California. Available at https://www.reaganlibrary.gov/research/speeches/52785a

Richard Nixon Pre-Presidential Materials, Richard Nixon Presidential Library and Museum, Yorba Linda, California.

Schaap, Dick. "Culture Shock." *New York Times,* September 28, 1975.

"Theme Index Museum Index 2016 Global Attractions Attendance Report." *Themed Entertainment Association.* Accessed May 5, 2018. http://www.teaconnect.org/images/files/TEA_235_103719_170601.pdf

Tuttle, Brittani "Flag retreat ceremonies return to Walt Disney World, Disneyland," *Attractions Magazine,* July 5, 2021, https://attractionsmagazine.com/flag-retreat-ceremonies-return-walt-disney-world-disneyland/

"We the People' Don't Know." *Sapulpa Daily Herald* [Sapulpa, OK], September 16, 1987.

"We the People" promotional flier. Political and Military History Collections, National Museum of American History, Smithsonian Institution.

White House Central Files, Richard Nixon Presidential Library and Museum, Yorba Linda, California.

Word, Ron. "Burger, Daniloff at Constitution Fete at Disney World." *Associated Press,* October 4, 1986. https://apnews.com/article/47e9c20ccfab6f07cfcb26d5e3ce2419

Wooten, James T. "Disney Will Join In Bicentennial." *New York Times,* February 19, 1975.

Winchell, Joan. "Disneyland, Revisited." *Los Angeles Times,* June 16, 1959.

"Wonderland Doors Open for Nixons." *The Choctaw Advocate,* February 9, 1956.

Woodyard, Chris. "Disneyland Offers Returning Troops 2 Free Tickets Each." *Los Angeles Times,* March 9, 1991.

Yothers, Jean. "30,000 See Wonders of Opening Day." *Orlando Sentinel,* October 25, 1971.

SECTION II

Negotiating American Identity at the Disney Parks

5
PROTEST AT THE PARKS: CHANGING AMERICA VIA DISNEY

One of the pillars of American democracy is the right of the citizens to petition their government. This can take many forms, including public demonstrations and protests. In the United States, there are certain recognized spaces for this type of engagement with the national narrative. Much like the agora in ancient Athens provided a public place for the dissent, protest, discussion and compromise that made the world's first democracy possible, open and civic spaces in American cities are frequently used as physical locations for the negotiation of the American national narrative.[1] The Disney theme parks play host (sometimes willingly, sometimes not) to the public's attempts to interact with or even shift the national narrative directly through demonstration or protest. Like groups that demonstrate in front of the White House or at state capitols, those who stage protests at a Disney theme park are coming to a space they believe represents the American people, and where their actions will garner attention from others. These types of events illustrate a crucial fact that many scholars overlook when discussing Disney's role in American identity: Disney Parks are not only locations that disseminate a narrative but are places where the public seeks to affect change in that narrative. They are not merely spaces where a corporation advances a vision of America that serves its capitalist purposes but are spaces, not unlike the National Mall or Lafayette Square in Washington, D.C., where the public attempts to grab the attention of the nation and its leaders, to call for shifts in historical narratives, and where people engage with one another to negotiate what it means to be an American.

Protests at the Parks

When a group of counter-culture free speech activists planned an "invasion" and "occupation" of Disneyland to protest U.S. involvement in the Vietnam

DOI: 10.4324/9781003315094-8

War, they unknowingly sparked a tradition of using Disney Park space for protest. August 6, 1970, marked the 50th anniversary of the dropping of the atomic bomb on Hiroshima, and a small group of California Yippies decided to use the anniversary to gain attention to their fight against the then-current war. "Yippies" were members of the Youth International Party, a group known for staging theatrical protests in order to grab attention to their free-speech, anti-war causes. The group had previously used platforms such as the Democratic National Convention, when they knew national media would be paying attention, to perform antics to "wake up" society to the strictures "the man" had them under. A few weeks before the anniversary, underground newspapers and fliers in California began advertising a "Yippie Day" at Disneyland. David Sacks, one of the organizers, created an attention-grabbing schedule of events for the day, including a "Black Panther breakfast at Aunt Jemima's Kitchen" in Frontierland a barbecue of Porky Pig (not even a Disney character) and a liberation of Minnie Mouse, later telling a blogger that it was obviously "pure fiction."[2] Around 300 "Yippies" showed up in the park that day, chanting as they made their way down Main Street, U.S.A., roving in small groups making the occasional counter-cultural remark or raising a power fist, climbing the rigging of a restaurant that resembled a pirate ship, until they finally "stormed Tom Sawyer's Island" and "ran up the Viet Cong flag" over the fort there.[3]

FIGURE 5.1 "Yippees" gather in a demonstration on Tom Sawyer's Island on August 6, 1970

Source: Courtesy of Jack Ricci.

While there were some minor scuffles between protestors and Anaheim police, it wasn't until a group tried to run the Yippie flag (which prominently featured a marijuana leaf) up a flagpole in Town Square, right next to an American flag, that there was a true confrontation between "straight" guests, as the press called non-Yippie visitors, and the Yippies. The symbolic raising of a counter-cultural flag directly next to the American flag was apparently too visual a call to shift traditional narratives for the more conservative crowd of visitors. The act caused one "straight" to object. Sacks later recalled that a man yelled, "How dare you raise that flag next to the American flag!" and so another Yippie "went to the other flagpole as this guy was trying to rip down the Yippie flag, and said, 'If you rip down our flag we'll rip down your flag.' He started to try to untie the American flag to bring it down. At which point fisticuffs broke out."[4] A cast member on duty that day, identified only as "Barry," reported a similar version of the incident, saying he "watched the ultimate—some Yippie trying to pull down the big American flag in Town Square and Dick Nunis, head of Disneyland, punch the guy in the face."[5] The incident of violence, which led to Disneyland closing six hours early and 23 arrests, is illustrative of how powerful the symbols and narratives we identify with are. It was the confrontation between the symbols that mattered to different groups of visitors that ultimately resulted in violence.

FIGURE 5.2 Anaheim police gather on Main Street, U.S.A., in the afternoon of August 6, 1970

Source: Courtesy of Jack Ricci.

Some of the Yippies told reporters that the choice of Disneyland was deliberate, not just for the attention they could garner but for what Disneyland represented: "It's a middle-class bastion," said one, "It's a plastic depiction of the American dream," said another.[6] "Man, that's America in there," reported one demonstrator.[7] The Yippies wanted to contrast the image of America Disneyland was portraying with the image that they wanted to see, not just at the theme park, but nationally. It was a sentiment that would be repeated through the years by demonstrators who looked to harness Disneyland's symbolic power to make points about American society and the national narrative writ large.

In the years since the Yippies "invaded," both Disneyland and Walt Disney World have seen a fair number of demonstrations, some meant to influence Disney specifically (particularly with regards to theme park labor practices), but many meant to influence the country. The demonstrations have ranged greatly in size and covered a variety of topics. The Yippies were an anti-war protest; in 2003 groups held up red, white, and blue signs outside of Disneyland's gates in support of a potential war in Iraq.[8] Demonstrations pushing for more accepting policies towards LGBTQ guests (discussed later in this chapter) have been contrasted with a group of Southern Baptists who handed fliers to Disneyland guests entering the park encouraging them to boycott Disney because of the company's extension of healthcare coverage to domestic partners of gay employees.[9] Protests have and continue to happen at both Disneyland and Walt Disney World. These examples all took place on the West Coast, but the East Coast park has also been the stage for protest ranging from animal rights groups against Disney's Animal Kingdom to activists who called for then-Disney CEO Bob Iger to renounce the business policies of President Donald Trump.[10]

Like the Yippies, protesting groups often explicitly claim their reasons for choosing Disney spaces for their protest are tied to their symbolic power and national platform. Though the Southern Baptist boycott was aimed at all Disney products worldwide, leader Pastor Wiley Drake stood outside Disneyland to protest because he felt the park represented "the heart of the whole issue."[11] The organizer of an anti-immigration protest in 2015, specifically speaking out against the use of H-1B visas by American companies to bring immigrant workers to the United States, chose to demonstrate at both Walt Disney World and Disneyland "because they're kind of the quintessential American business," and they hoped that other American businesses would take note of their protest because of Disney's status.[12] Again as the Yippies did, groups also directly connect their presence at a Disney Park to their desired changes in the country and a redefinition—or affirmation—of who and what is considered "American."

For several months in 2001, a small group of protesters from the Mexica Movement gathered outside of Disneyland every Saturday morning to protest a proposed Disney film in which Antonio Banderas was to play Emiliano Zapata. The group specifically protested because Banderas was Spanish, coming from a country that colonized Mexico, and yet had been cast as a Mexican leader. More broadly, they hoped to educate the country at large about indigenous Mexican culture and heritage within the United States, and for "Mexican-Americans to be recognized as American Indians also," claiming their space in America's narrative.[13]

In January 2018, a group of activists chose Disneyland's gates as a place to stake their claim directly to a piece of the American Experience. About 15 protestors staged a peaceful rally that temporarily blocked vehicle entrance to Disneyland. They were publicly demanding Congressional support for recipients of the Deferred Action for Childhood Arrivals program (DACA), commonly known as DREAMERS. One of the protesters, Barbara Hernandez, was told by her mother when she was six years old that they were going to Disneyland. This turned out to be code for the family moving to America.[14] Now, as an adult, Hernandez and her allies had chosen Disneyland as the stage for their protest because of its symbolic value, both as a representative space for America and because "it's where dreams come true." The protestors added, "But we're not on vacation anymore. We're still waiting for our dreams to come true."[15] Acknowledging the power of the Disney theme park as a location for public discourse and as an American symbol, the activists chose it as a place to engage in and publicize the national debate on who should be included in the national narrative.

Some demonstrations are smaller and less structured than organized protests. Individuals also react to the ways that Disney Parks tell the story of the United States. The Hall of Presidents at Walt Disney World, where every president from George Washington to the current commander-in-chief is represented in audio-animatronic form during a stirring, patriotic theatrical homage to the office and the country itself, regularly sees guests offering their opinion on the state of the American narrative via commentary on the presidents. Historically, guests have tended to interact with the figure of the sitting president in a negative fashion if unpopular. Bill Clinton was booed, and items were thrown at George W. Bush, for example, while they were in office. Richard Nixon is still occasionally booed when his figure is introduced. Individual presidential figures are often cheered or jeered (sometimes at the same time) reflecting the lenses through which audience members view them.[16] Guests often use their time in the queue to pass judgment on specific presidents and to teach their children the opinions they hold on them.[17] Though guests know, intellectually, that they are viewing robotic versions of the commander-in-chief, they sometimes can't help themselves from making commentary they don't have the opportunity to make in person.

A striking example of this followed the debut of the audio-animatronic of President Donald Trump in December 2017. The first public report of interaction came almost immediately. A video from December 27 showed a member of the crowd shouting "Lock him up!" during the Trump figure's speech, while another guest shouted back "He's not real!"[18] Regardless of Disney's intention for the figure, the mechanical Trump stands in as a Trump proxy for at least some members of the audience, which is one reason some feel it is a legitimate place to air their grievances. Jay Malsky, the 2017 Trump protestor put it best in his Twitter report of the incident: "I protested @realDonaldTrump at the #hallof-presidents cuz I'll never get this close in real life probs."[19]

Walt Disney intended for the Hall of Presidents to educate children about some of their nation's history, but over the years it has also come to function as a space for the public to express their opinion on the current administration and sometimes render a verdict on previous ones. Being one of the only places in the country where one can "face" all United States presidents at once makes the Hall of Presidents a powerful space for creating and expressing American collective memory.

These protest examples are in direct opposition to concerns on the part of some critics such as Henry Giroux, who worries that Disney's "corporate reach into everyday life ... will sanitize and trivialize any serious engagement with public memory, citizenship, and democracy."[20] In fact, Disney has increasingly become a place where the public goes to engage directly with questions of citizenship and democracy. In just one year, 2018, Disney Parks saw the DACA protest, a planned "die-in" at Walt Disney World to protest Disney's donations to a politician who supported the National Rifle Association (later canceled for fear of traumatizing children), and a man who unfurled a "Re-elect Trump" banner at Walt Disney World's Magic Kingdom Main Street Railroad and held up a "Trump 2020" placard for cameras while riding Splash Mountain.[21] In 2019, the same man moved his operation to Disneyland and dropped a "Trump 2020" banner from the side of the Mark Twain Riverboat.[22] These examples illustrate that protestors at Disney Parks articulate a mix of political views from conservative to liberal, in groups ranging in size from a hundred people to just one individual. Walt Disney once said, "At Disneyland, we are not Republican or Democrat—we are representing our country." Demonstrations at the Disney Parks are not just partisan, as in always "Republican" or "Democrat," but run the gamut of socially conservative to socially liberal issues.[23] The breadth of demonstration types and topics at Disney Parks mirrors that seen at traditional American public spaces used as locations of public engagement on social issues. The only significant difference is that these take place at a private location. When Walt Disney said Disneyland was "representing our country," he may not have envisioned it as a "bipartisan demonstration space" and yet, that's exactly what it has become.

Gay Days

One of the largest and most effective cultural demonstrations at the Disney Parks was begun less as a protest than as a simple statement of presence. Gay Days, today described on its website as "an all-over town, something-for-everyone vacation extravaganza," grew out of the desire of a group of Walt Disney World locals to gather with LGBTQ+ friends and allies for a fun day at the Magic Kingdom in 1991.[24] Their "fun day" would ultimately force the Disney Parks to take a public stance on whether or not they were welcoming of the LGBTQ+ community in their parks, a metaphorical statement that was nationally discussed and that helped to push the rest of America forward on a path of increased inclusion.[25]

Perhaps unknowingly, the Gay Days founders were replicating earlier gay activists at Disneyland in their "presence as protest" model. In 1980, a decade noted for its "increased visibility" of the gay community as a "cultural and political force in society," two young, gay men attempted to dance together at a Disneyland Date Night.[26] The original dance regulations still in place from 1957 allowed only for male–female pairs at the park's dance venues. The men were removed from the dance floor by security, and afterwards the men filed a lawsuit against the park alleging that their civil rights had been violated. The suit dragged on for four years, eventually culminating in a judge striking down the ban as it applied to the two men specifically. In 1985, Disneyland dropped the ban in its entirety.[27] A Disney spokesman at the time described the change as a response to teens wanting to dance with friends of the same sex at a newly opened dance club saying, "[W]e try to be responsive to the feedback we get from our guests." However, it was also clear to the LGBTQ+ community that the park was "finally paying attention to the world around them."[28] Whether the response on Disney's part was due to specific guest feedback, or by the fact that American culture had become more accepting (illustrated for Disney by those teens who weren't shy saying they wanted to dance with members of the same sex, whether friends or romantic partners), it not only represented a change on Disney property but helped the company to facilitate larger social change as well. In 1986, the Walt Disney Company sponsored its first charity event supporting the gay community, partnering with community groups in Orange County, California, to organize a benefit at Disneyland raising funds for AIDS Project Los Angeles. The company also pledged a charitable donation to match ticket sales.[29] By 1989, when Andrew Exler, one of the original Disneyland dancers who had filed suit in 1985, returned to dance with other male couples, guards again came up to them—this time to ensure that the crowds of other guests didn't give them any problems, a complete turnaround in attitude from nine years before.[30]

FIGURE 5.3 One of several celebratory buttons Exler and friends made at Disneyland on their return in 1989

Source: Courtesy of the National Museum of American History, Smithsonian Institution.

This change in company attitude was put to the test in 1991 when another "demonstration of presence" took place at Disney, this time in Walt Disney World's Magic Kingdom. Now known on both coasts as "Gay Days," the event began as a designated day, the first Saturday in June, where the LGBTQ+ community and its allies were encouraged to spend the day together enjoying each other's company in the Most Magical Place on Earth. Fliers for the event suggested attendees wear red t-shirts to better identify one another in the crowds. Though the event's founder, Doug Swallow, described the day as a time for the community to simply "have fun, to stand up and be counted," he clearly saw the potential for the moment as a demonstration, even tipping off a local newspaper beforehand.[31] As the event gained traction, its visibility grew, forcing Disney to acknowledge what they called a "large gathering of gays and lesbians inside" on signs they placed outside the Magic Kingdom on Gay Day 1992.[32] Disney at first acknowledged that the gathering might make some guests uncomfortable with signage and policies that allowed guests to get refunds for their tickets if they had unintentionally arrived on Gay Day, though they did not attempt to curtail the event, stating they "did not discriminate against anyone's right to visit the Magic Kingdom."[33] By 1996, Disney had stopped "warning" guests of Gay Days activities, with a spokesperson saying critics "made too much of just another day of magic," essentially acknowledging the acceptance and normalization of the LGBTQ+ community within Disney space, as well as the rest of society.[34]

Simultaneous to the Walt Disney World Gay Days demonstrations, LGBTQ+ and allied employees of The Walt Disney Company were advocating internally for support. The same year Gay Days began, the company worked with one of their cast members' unions to draft a policy that protected employees against discrimination on the basis of sexual preference.[35] Following from that, in 1995 they extended healthcare benefits to the partners and families of homosexual employees. They were among the early wave of American corporations to do so, which health insurance executives noted at the time "would likely spur corporate America [...] to consider health benefits for gay partners [...] I think other people will say, "if it's good enough for Disney, maybe it something we should consider."[36] This illustrated Disney's power to shift cultural norms, even when making what most would say was a business decision. From a simple assertion of presence at a Disney theme park flowed years of negotiations between the public and Disney to how the gay community was represented, mirroring and amplifying discussions taking place nationwide. This ongoing process has been effective, reflected in Disney's continued move towards more inclusive representation and America's continued moves toward acceptance and, increasingly, celebration, of the LGBTQ+ community.[37]

FIGURE 5.4 Attendees of Gay Days Anaheim 2021 pose in front of Sleeping Beauty Castle

Source: Courtesy of Eddie Shapiro.

Gay Days not only shows groups advocating effectively for larger change from Disney Parks—it also allows us to see groups advocating against said change, groups who, one could argue, were less successful. From its very first day, Gay Days had its share of counter-protestors, often small groups standing with placards or posters outside of the park, making comments to media outlets deriding the event and its participants. Protestors at the event were clearly fearful that the ultimate result of visible LGBTQ+ individuals in a Disney Park would be not just gay couples holding hands at Disney World but a national shift in American acceptance of the gay community, something they were actively against. One protestor claimed, "the agenda behind this is to desensitize the children and make them accept this lifestyle."[38] For several years groups such as "Operation Rescue" and the Southern Baptist Convention continued to protest both Gay Days and other instances of acceptance of the LGBTQ+ community on the part of Disney, such as the extension of healthcare to partners. Operation Rescue flew anti-LGBTQ banners over the Magic Kingdom and the Southern Baptist Convention sanctioned a Disney boycott by their members.[39] These counter-protests never grew to match the size or scope of Gay Days and have largely been forgotten today, while Gay Days itself continues to thrive.

The counter-protestors are an important part of considering Disney Parks as national locations because they illustrate that the parks' space is used by people on both sides of a debate as a space to capture the attention of the larger society. Like the National Mall, Disney is functioning as a stage from which people of varying beliefs appeal to leaders (of Disney, of the United States) and other citizens with their causes. Much like the nation itself, the Disney Parks allow for multiple points of view to be expressed before (most often) expressing the company's own support in one way or another for that which has come to be most reflective of the majority opinion in the United States. Disney Parks serve, then, as a nonpartisan democratic space, even while they are private space, making them important locations within the American identity landscape.

Flag Retreat

It is important to note that demonstrations are not always about calls to action to change the narrative. They can also affirm current cultural standards-hence they represent a true negotiation between past, present and future ideals. As noted in Chapter 4, both Disneyland and Walt Disney World have hosted nightly flag retreat ceremonies since their respective openings as a way for the company to honor America and her veterans. The ceremony has varied over time from a perfunctory retiring of the colors to a full ceremonial retreat. Its changing form and its endurance at Disneyland, specifically, has been influenced in part by one cast member and a group of citizens who "support and love the nightly Disneyland Flag Retreat ceremony" and whose advocacy for the retreat has had the effect of strengthening the already traditional patriotic experience.[40]

Gunnery Sergeant Ernest "Gunny" Napper retired from the United States Marine Corps in 1992 and immediately went to work as a security guard at Disneyland. As a veteran and American citizen, he felt moved by Disneyland's nightly flag retreat, though when he came on staff it was simple: a lowering of the colors with the national anthem playing on a boom box nearby. Napper noted that the ceremony "was important to me. And I know it was important to Mr. Disney too."[41] Indeed, it had been, with daughter Diane describing how Walt would "watch the flag lowering at Disneyland every evening [he and wife Lillian] were down there and tears would flow down his cheeks."[42] But in 1992, Napper didn't think Walt would be proud to watch the ceremony as it was then from his window. So, he created his own demonstration of sorts to bring attention to the ceremony, asking fellow cast members in costume—Mickey, Minnie, Snow White, whoever he could find—to gather with him around the flagpole in Town Square for the lowering, bringing together families eager to see the characters as well as the characters' own symbolic power as American symbols. Napper advocated tirelessly for the ceremony, and as word got out among the Disney community of regulars, the crowds grew. Disney eventually added the power of the Main Street Band and the Dapper Dans (a popular barbershop quartet) to the ceremony, and by the 2000s it had become so popular that crowds around the pole stood three people deep on Saturday evenings. Not only did guests from around the country come to take part in the ceremony, a group of locals, frequent visitors with annual passes, formed a support group of sorts, coming together every Saturday evening in Town Square to take part on behalf of veterans around the country, or as veterans themselves. The group went online in 2010 as the group "I Support the Disneyland Flag Retreat Ceremony" on Facebook, where they shared videos of the ceremony with people around the world, taking a Disneyland-specific American ritual and casting it worldwide.[43]

While most of the group's demonstration of support consists of showing up and taking part on a regular basis, they have occasionally raised their collective voice when Disney has attempted to alter what for them is an almost sacred tradition. For several years, the ceremony consisted of an entrance of the flag's honor guard (a group of Disneyland security cast members, often veterans themselves) accompanied by music from one of several Disneyland groups. Veterans were invited to stand around the flagpole and be recognized as the anthems from each military branch played. Before lowering the flag, the honor guard would verbally thank the veterans for their service. However, in 2015 Disney replaced the in-person thanks with a pre-recorded one that played over a loudspeaker, citing the need to ensure that all gathered could hear the message. The regular attendees were incredibly disappointed, having considered the personal touch to be one of the most respectful and meaningful parts of the cere-mony. "We posted on our Page and encouraged our members to email, write letters and call Disneyland and asked them to allow Gunny [and others] to continue to speak because it meant so much to Veterans," said "I Support the Disneyland Flag Retreat" co-founder Susan Emslie. "Well, there was such an outpouring of support within a day and a half Disneyland announced that Flag Retreat would continue to allow Gunny [and others] to speak."[44] The personal greetings continued until 2018, when Disney again opted for a pre-recorded message that said, "To all you have served our great nation, on behalf of the Disneyland Resort, we thank you for your honorable service to America."[45] Emslie called the recorded greeting "canned" and "im-personal," and the group again encouraged fans to petition Disney to return to the then-traditional format. Those who did received a response from Disney that the change was to provide a "more consistent Guest experience, and to ensure all Guests can hear the remarks."[46] Emslie and her group continue to support the retreat while continually lobbying for its increased prominence. They show up, they post on social media, they wear buttons of support, and they reach out to local media. "Retreat is a sacred time to those precious Veterans that faithfully gathered around The Pole to hear a faithful Veteran thank them. We will not give up the 'GOOD FIGHT.'"[47] The group sees preserving the ritual at Disneyland as a small way of preserving it in the nation at large, particularly when they share it on social media. They are explicitly using Disney Park space to influence the narrative, nationally, as one way to ensure that veterans are never forgotten. Their advocacy is less about affecting change to the national narrative than ensuring that parts of it, such as traditional forms of patriotic observance, remain, at Disneyland and beyond.

All these demonstrations and protests illustrate ways Disney theme parks pro-vide a space for collective participation and collaboration in shaping the national discourse. In some cases (such as, arguably, at the Hall of Presidents and at the Flag Retreat) Disney explicitly invites that participation, but more often the public takes it upon itself to initiate an interaction with the American narrative they see living at the parks. This keeps that narrative relevant to new generations, who can see themselves reflected in it and who can see ways to change it. It also suggests that the Disney-going public are not passive recipients of the narrative the park has built. They help to shape it, not merely through their consumer dollars, but through active participation. This interaction is the true evidence that Disney has taken its place as a location for not just the dissemination, but the negotiation of the American national narrative.

Notes

1 See Ashley Dunn, Constance McPhee and Allison Rudnick, "Art, Protest, and Public Space," *The Met*, October 2021, https://www.metmuseum.org/perspectives/articles/2021/10/art-protest-public-space and Peter Schwartzstein, "How Urban Design Can Make Or Break Protests," *Smithsonian Magazine*, July 29, 2020, https://www.smithsonianmag.com/history/geography-protest-how-urban-design-can-make-or-break-people-power-180975189/.
2 David Sacks, "Memories of a Yippie," *Davelandweb.com*, accessed December 13, 2021, https://www.davelandweb.com/yippies/.
3 Charles Powers and Bill Hazlett, "Yippies' Outburst Shuts Disneyland," *Los Angeles Times*, August 7, 1970, 1.
4 Sacks, "Memories."
5 Barry, "Memories of a Cast Member," *DavelandWeb.com*, accessed December 13, 2021, https://www.davelandweb.com/yippies/.
6 Associated Press, "Hippies Board Disneyland Pirate Ship," *The Hartford Courant*, August 7, 1970, 6.
7 Quoted in John M. Findlay, *Magic Lands: Western Cityscapes and American Culture After 1940* (Oakland, CA: University of California Press, 1992), 113.
8 Paul Wilborn, "Battle of Public Opinion Waged on Our Streets," *The Californian* [Temecula, CA], March 20, 2003, 5.
9 Associated Press, "Leader of boycott strikes Disneyland," *The Desert Sun* [Palm Springs, CA], July 13, 1997, 4.
10 Don Thomas, "Kingdom Opening Merriment Outweighs Animal Protest," *New York Beacon*, May 6, 1998, 26 and Deanna Ferrante, "Protest at Disney Tonight Calls for CEO Bob Iger to Leave Trump Advisory Council," *Orlando Weekly*, February 14, 2017, http://www.orlandoweekly.com/Blogs/archives/2017/02/14/protest-at-disney-tonight-calls-for-ceo-bob-iger-to-leave-trump-advisory-council.
11 Associated Press, "Leader of Boycott."
12 Sandra Pedicini, "Activists Plan Disney Protest Over Visa Issue," *The Orlando Sentinel*, October 7, 2015, A12.
13 V. Dion Haynes, "Natives Seek Distinction from Latinos," *Chicago Tribune*, May 21, 2001, 7.
14 Carlos Granada, "DACA Protest Temporarily Blocks Disneyland Entrance," *ABC* 7 (Los Angeles, CA), January 22, 2018, abc7.com/politics/daca-protest-temporarily-blocks-disneyland-entrance/2978429/. According to Smithsonian researcher Patricia Arteaga, it isn't uncommon for a "visit to Disneyland" to be used by Latinx immigrant families as a code for moving to the United States.
15 Branson-Potts, "DACA."
16 See, for instance, "Do people boo at Hall of Presidents," *Reddit*, accessed February 7, 2019, https://www.reddit.com/r/WaltDisneyWorld/comments/2tki1e/do_people_boo_at_hall_of_presidents/.
17 Mike Spata, "I sat through Disney's Hall of Presidents five times. It says more about us than Trump," *Tampa Bay Times*, February 18, 2018, https://www.tampabay.com/features/travel/attractions/I-sat-through-Disney-s-Hall-of-Presidents-five-times-It-says-more-about-us-than-Trump-_165255804/.

18 Ian R., "Fight Over Donald Trump at Disneyworld Hall of Presidents," Filmed [December 2017], YouTube video, 00:46, Posted [Dec. 27, 2017]. www.youtube. com/watch?time_continue=11&v=gwjOe5TK0BM.

19 Jay Malsky, Twitter Post, December 27, 2017, 6:34 p.m., https://twitter.com/ jaymalsky/status/946147176488546304?lang=en.

20 Henry Giroux, *The Mouse That Roared: Disney and the End of Innocence* (Lanham, MD: Rowman & Littlefield Publishers, Inc., 2010), 79.

21 Gray Rohrer, "Disney 'Die-In' Protest Canceled to Avoid 'Trauma' to Kids," *Orlando Sentinel*, June 25, 2018. https://www.orlandosentinel.com/news/politics/political-pulse/os-disney-die-in-canceled-20180625-story.html, Aris Folley, "Man sneaks 'Re-Elect Trump' Banner into Disney World's Magic Kingdom," *The Hill*, September 24, 2018. https://thehill.com/blogs/blog-briefing-room/news/408127-man-installs-re-elect-trump-banner-at-walt-disney-worlds-magic and Kalham Rosenblatt, "Disney World Bans Man Who Held Trump Sign on Splash Mountain," *NBC News*, November 14, 2018. https://www.nbcnews.com/news/us-news/disney-world-bans-man-who-held-trump-sign-splash-mountain-n936151.

22 David Brennan, "Video: Man Hangs Trump 2020 Banner at Disneyland, Gets Thrown Out After Another "Operationflagdrop," *Newsweek*, February 14, 2019, https://www. newsweek.com/video-man-hangs-trump-2020-banner-disneyland-gets-thrown-out-after-another-1331113.

23 Walt Disney quoted in Marcy Carriker Smothers, *Walt's Disneyland: A Walk in the Park with Walt Disney* (Los Angeles: Disney Editions, 2021), 36.

24 The Walt Disney Company has a long and complicated history with regards to its relationship to the LGBTQ+ community, one which parallels the long and complicated history of America in general to that community. The most definitive overview text of this relationship is Sean Griffin, *Tinker Belles and Evil Queens: The Walt Disney Company from the Inside Out* (New York University Press, 2000). "Guide to the Official Gay Days," *GayDays.com*, accessed December 7, 2021, https://www.gaydays.com/index.php/guide-to-gay-days.

25 See Bethanee Bemis, "A Cartoon City Upon a Hill" in *Mediating the Mouse: Disney and the Fan Experience*, ed. Priscilla Hobbs (Bristol, UK: Intellect Ltd., 2022).

26 Griffin, *Tinker Belles*, 133.

27 Maria La Ganga, "Disneyland Drops Policy Prohibiting Same-sex Dancing," *Los Angeles Times,* August 14, 1985, OC_A1.

28 La Ganga, "Disneyland Drops."

29 Griffin, *Tinker Belles,* 190–191.

30 Associated Press, "Disney Takes Same-Sex Dancing in Stride," *Journal Gazette* [Matoon, Illinois], September 20, 1989, C3.

31 Bob Morris, "Gays and Lesbians Plan Day at Disney," *Orlando Sentinel*, June 3, 1991, https://www.orlandosentinel.com/news/os-xpm-1991-06-03-9106030289-story.html and Jeff Truesdell, "How Gay Days Pushed Disney Out of the Closet," *Orlando Weekly*, May 31, 2000, https://www.orlandoweekly.com/orlando/how-gay-day-pushed-disney-out-of-the-closet/Content?oid=2262655.

32 Truesdell, "How Gay Days."

33 Truesdell, "How Gay Days."

34 "Gay Day Was Ahead of Its Time, and Has Been Filled with Surprises Ever Since," *Watermark Online*, May 27, 2010, http://www.watermarkonline.com/2010/05/27/ gay-day-was-ahead-of-its-time-and-has-been-filled-with-surprises-since.

35 Chris Woodyard, "Disney Pledges Not to Discriminate on Sexual Preference," *Los Angeles Times*, November 7, 1991.

36 Chris Woodyard, "Disney to Give," *Los Angeles Times*, October 7, 1995.

37 Statistically, Americans' acceptance and support of homosexuality and LGBTQ+ individuals has been steadily rising since the 1980s, demonstrating that Disney's stance is firmly in line with social trends. In 2018, Disney introduced rainbow-themed merchandise to coincide with Pride month and Gay Days, and in 2019 they sold their first

official celebratory Pride collection. See "Attitudes on Same-Sex Marriage," *Pew Research Center*, May 14, 2019, https://www.pewforum.org/fact-sheet-changing-attitudes-on-gay-marriage.

38 "Disney World Is Wary Site of Gay Party," *New York Times*, June 5, 1994, 28.

39 "Operation Rescue Quietly Protests Gay Day at Disney World," *CNN*, June 6, 1998, http://www.cnn.com/US/9806/06/disney.protest/index.html, and Mark Pinsky, *The Gospel According to Disney: Faith, Trust, and Pixie Dust* (Louisville: Westminster John Knox Press, 2004), 253.

40 Sean Emslie, "I Support the Disneyland Flag Retreat Ceremony," Facebook, December 6, 2021, https://www.facebook.com/groups/dlflagretreat/.

41 Dennis McCarthy, "Retired Marine Ernie Napper Adds Life to Disneyland's flag retreat," *Los Angeles Daily News*, November 7, 2013, https://www.dailynews.com/2013/11/07/retired-marine-ernie-napper-adds-life-to-disneylands-flag-retreat/.

42 Diane Disney Miller quoted in Smothers, 36.

43 As of December 2021 the group has over 6,200 members.

44 Susan Emslie, Facebook messenger exchange with Bethanee Bemis, December 7, 2021.

45 Tom Bell, "Fans Not Happy About Changes to Disneyland's Flag Retreat Ceremony," *Disney Information Station*, February 27, 2018, https://www.wdwinfo.com/news-stories/fans-not-happy-about-changes-to-disneylands-flag-retreat-ceremony/.

46 Bell, "Fans Not."

47 Emslie, Facebook messenger, 2021.

References

"Attitudes on Same-Sex Marriage." *Pew Research Center*, May 14, 2019. https://www.pewforum.org/fact-sheet-changing-attitudes-on-gay-marriage

Associated Press. "Disney Takes Same-Sex Dancing in Stride." *Journal Gazette* [Matoon, Illinois], September 20, 1989.

Associated Press. "Hippies Board Disneyland Pirate Ship." *The Hartford Courant*, August 7, 1970.

Associated Press. "Leader of Boycott Strikes Disneyland," *The Desert Sun* [Palm Springs, CA], July 13, 1997.

Barry. "Memories of a Cast Member." *DavelandWeb.com*. Accessed December 13, 2021. https://www.davelandweb.com/yippies/

Bell, Tom. "Fans Not Happy About Changes to Disneyland's Flag Retreat Ceremony." *Disney Information Station*, February 27, 2018, https://www.wdwinfo.com/news-stories/fans-not-happy-about-changes-to-disneylands-flag-retreat-ceremony/

Bemis, Bethanee. "A Cartoon City Upon a Hill." In *Mediating the Mouse: Disney and the Fan Experience*, edited by Priscilla Hobbs. Bristol, UK: Intellect Ltd., 2022.

Branson-Potts, Hailey and Cindy Carcamo. "DACA Recipients Temporarily Block Disneyland Entrance as an Act of Civil Disobedience." *LA Times*, 22 January 22, 2018. http://www.latimes.com/local/lanow/la-me-ln-disneyland-daca-protest-20180122-htmlstory.html

Brennan, David. "Video: Man Hangs Trump 2020 Banner at Disneyland, Gets Thrown Out After Another "Operationflagdrop." *Newsweek*, February 14, 2019. https://www.newsweek.com/video-man-hangs-trump-2020-banner-disneyland-gets-thrown-out-after-another-1331113

"Disney World Is Wary Site of Gay Party." *New York Times*, June 5, 1994.

"Do People Boo at Hall of Presidents." *Reddit*. Accessed February 7, 2019. https://www.reddit.com/r/WaltDisneyWorld/comments/2tki1e/do_people_boo_at_hall_of_presidents/

Dunn, Ashley, Constance McPhee and Allison Rudnick. "Art, Protest, and Public Space." *The Met*, October 2021. https://www.metmuseum.org/perspectives/articles/2021/10/art-protest-public-space

Ferrante, Deanna. "Protest at Disney Tonight Calls for CEO Bob Iger to Leave Trump Advisory Council." *Orlando Weekly*, February 14, 2017. http://www.orlandoweekly.com/Blogs/archives/2017/02/14/protest-at-disney-tonight-calls-for-ceo-bob-iger-to-leave-trump-advisory-council

Findlay, John M. *Magic Lands: Western Cityscapes and American Culture After 1940*. Oakland, CA: University of California Press, 1992.

Folley, Aris. "Man sneaks 'Re-Elect Trump' banner into Disney World's Magic Kingdom." *The Hill*, September 24, 2018. https://thehill.com/blogs/blog-briefing-room/news/408127-man-installs-re-elect-trump-banner-at-walt-disney-worlds-magic

"Gay Day was ahead of its time, and has been filled with surprises ever since," *Watermark Online*, May 27, 2010. http://www.watermarkonline.com/2010/05/27/gay-day-was-ahead-of-its-time-and-has-been-filled-with-surprises-since

Giroux, Henry. *The Mouse That Roared: Disney and the End of Innocence*. Lanham, MD: Rowman & Littlefield Publishers, Inc., 2010.

Granada, Carlos. "DACA Protest Temporarily Blocks Disneyland Entrance." *ABC 7* (Los Angeles, CA), January 22, 2018. abc7.com/politics/daca-protest-temporarily-blocks-disneyland-entrance/2978429/

Griffin, Sean. *Tinker Belles and Evil Queens: The Walt Disney Company from the Inside Out*. New York University Press, 2000.

"Guide to the Official Gay Days" *GayDays.com*. Accessed December 7, 2021. https://www.gaydays.com/index.php/guide-to-gay-days

Haynes, V. Dion. "Natives Seek Distinction from Latinos." *Chicago Tribune*, May 21, 2001.

Ian, R. "Fight Over Donald Trump at Disneyworld Hall of Presidents." Filmed [December 2017]. YouTube video. 00:46. Posted [December 27, 2017]. www.youtube.com/watch?time_continue=11&v=gwjOe5TK0BM

La Ganga, Maria. "Disneyland Drops Policy Prohibiting Same-Sex Dancing." *Los Angeles Times*, August 14, 1985.

Malsky, Jay. Twitter Post. December 27, 2017. 6:34 p.m. https://twitter.com/jaymalsky/status/946147176488546304?lang=en

McCarthy, Dennis. "Retired Marine Ernie Napper Adds Life to Disneyland's Flag Retreat." *Los Angeles Daily News*, November 7, 2013. https://www.dailynews.com/2013/11/07/retired-marine-ernie-napper-adds-life-to-disneylands-flag-retreat/

Morris, Bob. "Gays and Lesbians Plan Day at Disney." *Orlando Sentinel*, June 3, 1991. https://www.orlandosentinel.com/news/os-xpm-1991-06-03-9106030289-story.html

"Operation Rescue Quietly Protests Gay Day at Disney World." *CNN*, June 6, 1998. http://www.cnn.com/US/9806/06/disney.protest/index.html

Pinsky, Mark. *The Gospel According to Disney: Faith, Trust, and Pixie Dust*. Louisville: Westminster John Knox Press, 2004.

Pedicini, Sandra. "Activists Plan Disney Protest Over Visa Issue." *The Orlando Sentinel*, October 7, 2015.

Powers, Charles and Bill Hazlett. "Yippies' Outburst Shuts Disneyland." *Los Angeles Times*, August 7, 1970.

Rohrer, Gray. "Disney 'Die-In' Protest Canceled to Avoid 'Trauma' to Kids." *Orlando Sentinel*, June 25, 2018. https://www.orlandosentinel.com/news/politics/political-pulse/os-disney-die-in-canceled-20180625-story.html

Rosenblatt, Kalham. "Disney World Bans Man Who Held Trump Sign on Splash Mountain" *NBC News*, November 14, 2018. https://www.nbcnews.com/news/us-news/disney-world-bans-man-who-held-trump-sign-splash-mountain-n936151

Sacks, David. "Memories of a Yippie." *Davelandweb.com*. Accessed December 13, 2021. https://www.davelandweb.com/yippies/

Schwartzstein, Peter. "How Urban Design Can Make or Break Protests." *Smithsonian Magazine*, July 29, 2020. https://www.smithsonianmag.com/history/geography-protest-how-urban-design-can-make-or-break-people-power-180975189/

Sean Emslie, Sean. "I Support the Disneyland Flag Retreat Ceremony." Facebook, December 6, 2021, https://www.facebook.com/groups/dlflagretreat/

Smothers, Marcy Carriker. *Walt's Disneyland: A Walk in the Park with Walt Disney*. Los Angeles: Disney Editions, 2021.

Spata, Mike. "I Saw Through Disney's Hall of Presidents Five Times. It Says More About Us Than Trump." *Tampa Bay Times*, February 18, 2018. https://www.tampabay.com/features/travel/attractions/I-sat-through-Disney-s-Hall-of-Presidents-five-times-It-says-more-about-us-than-Trump-_165255804/

Thomas, Don. "Kingdom Opening Merriment Outweighs Animal Protest." *New York Beacon*, May 6, 1998.

Truesdell, Jeff. "How Gay Days Pushed Disney Out of the closet." *Orlando Weekly*, May 31, 2000. https://www.orlandoweekly.com/orlando/how-gay-day-pushed-disney-out-of-the-closet/Content?oid=2262655

Wilborn, Paul. "Battle of Public Opinion Waged on Our Streets." *The Californian* [Temecula, CA], March 20, 2003.

Woodyard, Chris. "Disney Pledges Not to Discriminate on Sexual Preference." *Los Angeles Times*, November 7, 1991.

Woodyard, Chris. "Disney to Give," *Los Angeles Times*, October 7, 1995.

6

RETHEMING: VISUALIZING A CHANGING AMERICA AT DISNEY PARKS

A major factor in the Disney theme parks' ability to remain relevant for over 60 years as places of collective memory of the national narrative is that they adjust the narrative they present to reflect changes in prevailing cultural attitudes. At the same time, the company has kept the narrative static enough and slow enough to respond to those attitude changes that the parks' presentation remains familiar and appealing to multiple generations. In this way, the narrative changes while not seeming jarring to different generations of visitors. The previous chapter looked at ways in which the public uses Disney theme parks to affect larger social change; this chapter discusses how the changing demographics and ideals of the public outside of Disney's gates have a direct impact on physical Disney spaces, and thus on Disney's portrayal of our national narrative. Further, it suggests that physical change at the Disney Parks can be read as indicative of larger cultural shifts within the American identity landscape—by the time society has shifted enough to trigger change at a Disney theme park, that shift can be considered dominant or mainstream.

Former head of Imagineering and co-worker of Walt Disney Marty Sklar once related that Walt believed the Disneyland concept was successful "because it answered the needs of the people."[1] Walt was speaking specifically of a public desire for family-friendly entertainment, but there is much more to it than that. The Disney Parks' meet guests' physical needs with abundant food stands and restrooms, their needs for entertainment with just about everything they offer, and their needs for safe play spaces with their attention to security. Beyond that, they meet deeper, cultural needs, such as the need for a shared social institution, and the need for a unifying mythology. Through changing the face of that unifying mythology with physical park updates, Disney is also meeting the public's need to adapt its own identity and history. As Linda Small has written, "a populace engaged in reconstituting its social personal creates a mythical history and image capable of incorporating the meaning of their past experience into the present

DOI: 10.4324/9781003315094-9

cultural matrix."[2] Each time there is a shift in the American social persona, whether relating to public health, understanding of shared histories, or increased participation of different minority groups in the larger social sphere, Americans push, both consciously and unconsciously, to see that reflected in their cultural matrix, in this case, as filtered through the Disney Parks. Americans send a message to Disney (and others) every time they make a purchase, consume one type of media over another, vote in elections, or interact on social media. The message is, at any given time, in the aggregate: we like this and not that, we *believe* this and not that, we *are* this and not that.

Our choices, based on our likes and dislikes, translate into messages about who we are socially, about our identity, and about the values we collectively lay claim to. For example, the box office and critical success of the 2016 film *Moana* and the 2017 film *Coco*, both films centered on characters of color, were understood by many as proof that Americans were increasingly valuing inclusion and diversity in their daily lives, including their entertainment.[3] The commercial success of the films led directly to their physical inclusion in the Disney theme parks, not only in transient walk-around character appearances but in semipermanent installations. For example, a scene inspired by *Coco* was incorporated into the Magic Kingdom "Mickey's Philharmagic" attraction in 2021 and a Moana-themed attraction called "Journey of Water" was under construction at Epcot the same year.[4] This is evidence that the Disney company pays attention to the desires of their customer and translates those desires into physical changes in the representation of American values at Disney Parks. In 2014 then-Senior Vice President at Disney Parks and Resorts Tom Boyles told attendees at a brand experience symposium, "Disney Parks and Resorts exist to make magical experiences come alive ... A good part of doing this is knowing your guest well enough to be relevant to them. In 2010, we set the goal to be relevant to every guest, every day, every time they interacted with our brand."[5] Through knowing the guests, letting the guests say what is important to them, and by repeating that back, Disney echoes and reinforces culture and identity, as they have been, and as they are becoming.

American identity has been evolving since it came into existence, and since their creation, Disney theme parks have evolved alongside it. Some shifts have garnered seemingly little public attention, perhaps because the level of social acceptance for such change was already overwhelming. Park policies on certain social 'vices' have shifted as their level of acceptance in the general public has changed: alcohol was once banned on park property (except for the private Club 33), but it is now served to a public eager to consume it in multiple locations at both Disneyland and Walt Disney World. When Epcot opened in 1982 its selling of alcohol was somewhat controversial; now the concept known as "drinking around the world," where guests consume an alcoholic beverage in each of the 11 different pavilions in Epcot's World Showcase is so popular many vendors sell t-shirts promoting it.[6] Where smoking was once allowed at Disney Parks, its acceptance was narrowed first to specific locations, then banned altogether as the tolerance of second-hand smoke has become all but nonexistent in the rest of America.[7]

Disney's policy on fake guns in the parks has continually shifted as the nation continues to debate their place in our narrative. Toy rifles that once were used by children playacting as Tom Sawyer and Huck Finn were removed from Fort Langhorn on Tom Sawyer's Island at Disneyland (the attraction later closed altogether) but remain at Walt Disney World as of this writing. Skippers on the Jungle Cruise ride have occasionally been discouraged from discharging the guns kept at the front of the boat for a comedic bit in which the skippers frighten away menacing hippos by firing blanks into the air.[8] While both Walt Disney World and Disneyland still feature shooting arcades where visitors may shoot replica .54-caliber Hawkins buffalo rifles over the historical landscape of Boot Hill in Tombstone, Arizona, the guns do not fire projectiles—they utilize laser beam technology to hit infrared targets.[9] The comments of two visitors at Disney World in 2002 illustrate the way in which guns continue to exist in a difficult cultural landscape in the United States. When asked to comment on the fact that toy guns were sold at Walt Disney World but not Disneyland, one guest said, "Disney prides itself in supporting traditional family values. It should set a better example," while another commented, "They are presented here as an important part of American history … We can't deny our past, in which firearms played an important part." While some see firearms as an important part of American history, some view it as the antithesis of what American families stand for. As both attitudes continue to exist in America, Disney finds itself walking a cultural line—selling toy guns to those who wish to purchase them but using lasers instead of bullets in play guns meant to be fired within the park.[10]

Dress policies for cast members have also been updated several times as the social traits stereotypically associated with certain looks have changed. "The Disney Look," states the appearance standards set forth for Disney employees at any given time. In 2019 it was described on the Disney Careers website as "a classic look that is clean, natural, polished and professional, and avoids 'cutting edge' trends or extreme styles," a description that has been true since Disneyland's opening.[11] For many years, male cast were required to have short hair and be clean-shaven. No long-haired male guests were allowed either; the lack of a haircut was considered by 1950s Disneyland executives as a possible signifier of someone interested in social disruption. However, as Disney historian David Koenig told the *Los Angeles Times,* "What was clean cut in the 1950s isn't quite the same today."[12] No longer considered a signature look of civil disobedience in the general population, in 2021 male and female cast hair length is at their discretion, though hair must be "clean and well maintained."[13] For years the Disney Look prohibited any visual tattoos, but with statistics showing almost half of those between the ages of 18 and 34 have at least one tattoo, Disney adjusted its guidelines in 2021 to allow cast to show moderately sized tattoos of an "appropriate" nature, a decision born of both the company's desire to create a more inclusive workplace and the need to retain good workers.[14]

More significant than these changes that have evolved in relatively small ways over time, so subtle that they are often noticed only by the frequent Disney visitor or media outlets, is Disney's changing representation of women and minority groups at their theme parks. These changes often garner more widespread attention in ways that shine a light on larger shifts within American attitudes in general.

Diversity at the Disney Parks

The question of how well Disney Park narratives reflect the true diversity of America has been continually asked over the past six decades.[15] How comprehensive was Walt Disney's opening day proclamation that Disneyland would offer welcome "to *all* who come to this happy place" or Roy Disney's dedication hope that Walt Disney World would bring joy, inspiration and knowledge to *all*? The national narrative reflected in the early Disney theme parks catered to an American population that was 89.3% white in 1950, both because the majority of early park consumers came from that population and because Disneyland's original creators themselves were working from largely white, male, middle-class lived experience.[16]

But that meant the Disney Parks in their original forms often left out the narratives of non-white Americans or told them from an outsider's point of view. Even before it was officially opened, reporters at the *Miami Herald* leveled criticism at Walt Disney World for being too "representative of the Middle American upbringing of Disney himself."[17]

In 2021, the American population is more diverse than ever before and only predicted to become more so. The changing face of America is pushing the country to question its traditional narratives and shift from the white-centric national narrative seen in the 1950s to one that better reflects the experiences of Americans today. On an official, federal level, there has been a decade-long push to diversify National Historic Sites and National Parks, resulting in new parks focused on minority experience, such as the Harriet Tubman Underground Railroad National Historic Park, and expanded interpretation at natural history sites, such as that at Mammoth Cave National Park in Kentucky, which today includes information on the first park guides, who were enslaved black men.[18] The Smithsonian Institution opened the National Museum of the American Indian in 2004, the National Museum of African American History and Culture in 2016, and in 2020 was authorized by Congress to create the National Museum of the American Latino and the Smithsonian American Women's History Museum, shaping the physical way America's story is represented in the nation's capital as more diverse and welcoming.

Examples of how the Disney theme parks' have physically changed to accommodate this blossoming national narrative of inclusion are illustrative of how the theme parks are situated alongside these official national places of commemoration as places of importance to the American experience, akin to the official places themselves.[19]

Women Through the Disney Park Lens

Women have always been present in the landscape of the Disney Parks, as cast members, as audio-animatronic characters, as images featured in-park experiences and entertainment. The way in which they are interpreted and featured, however, has undergone revision.

By the 1840s, men and women in the United States were understood to inhabit separate spheres—men in the world of work and women in domestic life. Alexis de Tocqueville, in his study *Democracy in America*, identified the division of roles by sex as a distinctly American trait. Whether or not this was more theory or a reality, the *idea* of male and female spheres continued as a narrative of American life.[20] It was particularly strong in the 1950s, when Disneyland was conceived, as post-World War II society sought to push women who had found work outside the home during wartime back into the domestic sphere and out of jobs that returning GIs might otherwise occupy. Presentation of women at the Disney Parks during their first decades often saw women either left out entirely or situated in prescribed spheres. However, as the second, third and fourth waves of feminism rolled across the United States, they brought change in how Americans think about women's roles historically and in present society, adjusting both the nation's narratives surrounding women and the narratives presented on Disney property.[21]

In the early decades of the park, Disneyland cast members were relegated to certain work spheres based on sex, with "frilly-frocked females working Storybook Land and macho men in pith helmets wisecracking through the Jungle Cruise."[22] Traditionally, only men were cast in "driving" roles, including Jungle Cruise skipper, train engineer, Omnibus operator or steamboat captain. Only women were cast in "storytelling" roles such as Storybook Land Canal Boat guides and Tiki Room hostesses. Disney archivist Dave Smith ties the gendered casting directly to the role of women in popular culture at the time of Disneyland's creation, likening Storybook boat guides to June Cleaver telling bedtime stories and Jungle Cruise skippers to Humphrey Bogart in "The African Queen," the film on which the ride was initially modeled.[23]

This casting by sex held out at Disneyland until 1995, when a female cast member, Suzanne Barnaby, returned from a Walt Disney World vacation having noted that the East Coast park featured female skippers and asked to be allowed to occupy the same position. According to attractions supervisor Bruce Kimbrell, the park had in fact "experimented" with female skippers before, in 1974 and again in 1987. The experiment was declared a failure in the 1970s due to, as Kimbrell described it, the public's unwillingness to "accept women daredevils" and in the 1980s because of what attractions director Craig Smith deemed problems "from a female perspective," meaning women found it difficult to "load guests and push boats around."[24] Interestingly, both Kimbrell and Smith spoke from a male, managerial perspective that might not have reflected the female skipper's actual experiences.[25] Regardless of why it happened, the fact that women were pushed out of the previously identified male role in the 1970s and 1980s parallels historical trends in the culture at large. The 1970s push by feminists for ratification of the Equal Rights Amendment saw serious conservative pushback, and the 1980s, dominated by political conservatism, have been labeled by some as an age of "backlash against women."[26] However, as third-wave feminism rose in the 1990s and women once again sought increasing agency in their own lives, the combination of women like Barnaby asserting their desire for the skipper role and the increased acclimatization of the country to "female daredevils" (for example, in jobs such as fighter pilot and entertainment roles such as sidekicks in the Indiana Jones trilogies), the 1995 switch to gender-inclusive Jungle Cruise skippers held fast. This change also helped to desegregate other park roles, with women canoeing to Tom Sawyer Island and piloting the Mark Twain riverboat. Kimbrell declared that going forward "there [would] be no barriers" of sex to Disney cast members.[27]

In addition to live women, audio-animatronic ones were also given roles based on gender. While women were present as figures along the boat ride Pirates of the Caribbean from its first voyage in 1967, they were all cast as victims of pirates pillaging a Caribbean town. The light-hearted tone of the ride seemingly made light of their suffering from sex trafficking and violence. For the first 30 years of its run, Pirates riders cruised past scenes of male pirates chasing women in circles, intent on grabbing them (presumably for sexual violence and exploitation), an auction scene in which women were roped together being sold into what can only be inferred is sexual slavery and a particularly disturbing scene where a character known as the "Pooped Pirate" or "Gluttonous Pirate" waved a woman's petticoat and said, "It's sore I be to hoist me colors upon the likes of that shy little wench … I be willing to share, I be," while the terrified object of his lust hid in a barrel nearby.[28]

While this portrayal may have been historically accurate, because of its location at the Disney Parks the lens through which this ride present women can appear to represent the perspective of the entire country in the present. Therefore, when it became apparent the Pirates of the Caribbean ride was out of step with the views of many of the American people, the company stepped in to adjust it. Thus, simultaneously, as third-wave feminism rejected the framing of women as victims and objects used and abused by a patriarchal society and sought female agency both in their own lives and in how women were depicted in history and entertainment, Disney responded to complaints regarding this ride's depiction of women as victims of sexual violence and altered some of the scenes. In 1997 the men chasing women and the "Gluttonous Pirate" were edited so that the object of their lust appeared to be food, with some of them chasing women now holding platters of food and drink, and others being chased away by women holding broomsticks. The "Gluttonous Pirate" now proclaims himself full of food—"Me belly be feeling like a galleon with a load of treasure"—while being watched not by a terrified girl but a cat.[29]

In 2018, the scene in which women were auctioned off as "brides" was updated to an auction of goods by the ride's first female pirate. The new pirate, Redd, is a reimaging of the redheaded "bride" who had "delighted" pirates in the previous auction scene, who shouted "We wants the redhead! We wants the redhead!" The other women in the scene appear to gain at least some agency as well by bringing goods to the auction. Whether they bring them willingly or by force is unknown, but they themselves appear to have escaped a potentially horrific fate. A Disney fan site noted that while not all fans were pleased with the changes, most could see how the move "embod[ied] the evolving nature of the parks and the history the Disneyland Resort has of remaining relevant with modern culture trends."[30] One fan summed up the relationship between the change and the culture it reflected, saying:

> Disneyland needs to reflect the times, and it seems to me this is the time to change it ... It's uncomfortable even for me [as a male] to see women being sold into bondage and human trafficking. I can't even imagine what little girls think about this. It seems to me that Disney was just ahead of the curve on all this 'Me Too' movement, because they announced this change last summer.'[31]

The "Me Too" movement in the United States, a social movement against sexual harassment and abuse, was strong on social media in 2017 and 2018. While Disney had announced the changes to Pirates before the movement's hashtag went viral, the physical changes came during the height of the protest, a possible sign that Disney's read on social trends is not merely reactionary, but predictive.

These 2018 updates to Pirates came a few years before another update to the Jungle Cruise that centers the story of the ride around a woman of color: Alberta Falls, owner of the Jungle Navigation Company that runs the popular cruises, a woman of British and Indian ancestry. The timing of the Jungle Cruise update, taken together with the timing of the first Pirates gender role updates, clearly indicates Disney's decisions were responses to waves of feminism influencing how Americans want women to be understood in the larger national narrative. While the updates of the 1990s focus on themes of third-wave feminism, giving women agency and roles other than "victim" or "passive hostess," the updates of 2017–2021 can be tied to fourth-wave feminism, in the way that they focus on inclusivity beyond gender: Alberta Falls is identified as being biracial and Redd occupies a space historically associated with women who might today claim identities along the LGBTQ spectrum.[32]

Minority Representation on Disney Landscapes

The inclusion of Alberta Falls in the Jungle Cruise is one of the most recent changes to how people of color are portrayed on Disney property. The history of racial minority representation at Disney, like that of women, parallels changes in how those minorities have been included or excluded in the national narrative.

Many of the most overtly racist and problematic attractions in Disney Park history were updated in the 1960s and 1970s, coinciding with the Civil Rights Movement which was calling for re-evaluation of the roles of American minority groups in the larger society. The lens with which 1950s Disneyland viewed minority groups in American history, particularly persons of color, fit with the public civics education views of the time period that used history to justify American imperialism (especially as the America outside of Disney's gates was justifying entry into other countries, often uninvited, as necessary fights against the global evils of communism). In other words, minorities may have been present, but they weren't an integral part of the story, and further, the individuals themselves were represented as being content with that role.[33] For example, American Indian presence was not integrated in spaces representing the future (Tomorrowland) or fantasy (Fantasyland), but rather relegated to the historical Frontierland in the forms of an Indian Village, or Main Street, U.S.A., in the form of a "Cigar Store Indian" statue.

The Indian Village has a complicated legacy. Disneyland had attempted to "faithfully recreate" a Plains Indian experience, utilizing "tribal consultants," staffing the village with American Indian actors and allowing them to bring their own regalia as their on-stage costumes, but the results were problematic in many ways. According to "Disneyland Village Chief" Shooting Star (Louis Heminger, a Dakota Sioux tribe member) the space was "dedicated to the preservation of Indian traditions and customs," and included "animal hide tepees, birch bark council houses, ceremonial dances, war canoes the visitor can paddle, and real Indians," with an Indian War Canoe ride, where guests paddled along with two American Indian guides and scenes of "friendly" and "unfriendly" Indian villages along the track of the Disneyland railroad.[34] The village was a composite of at least 10 different tribal traditions and actors, suggesting that they were interchangeable with one another. Setting the village up as an attraction to be viewed by largely white audiences, accessible through a tunnel and lying in a corner of the park, created a sense of American Indians as "other," rather than part of American life in both past and present—in fact, a Russian newspaper referred to the village as a place where Disney kept "a tribe of American Indians in captivity, to amuse visitors." The Indian War Canoes both suggest that the indigenous peoples were hostile towards "real" Americans, white settlers, and were staffed with what promotional literature referred to as "Indian braves," which, while Disney billed it as showcasing indigenous craft, could also be interpreted as placing American Indians once again as subservient to white audiences. Disney literature in 1967 claimed that the purpose of the village was "to erase a long-held impression here and abroad that all Indians are war-whooping savages capable of little else than forever galloping across television and movie screens" yet the Village presented very much as a movie set.[35] The Indian Village closed and the Indian War Canoe ride was renamed to Davy Crockett's Explorer Canoes in 1971 (often staffed by cast members in coonskin caps as opposed to "Indian braves"). These changes came two years after the occupation of Alcatraz by American Indian activists brought national attention to the Red Power movement for indigenous self-determination.[36]

Aunt Jemima's Pancake House, when it opened in 1955, was the only Disneyland attraction with a person of color at the center of its story. It featured an actress,

Ayelene Lewis, portraying a stereotypical Mammy character, Aunt Jemima, who was apparently quite content to serve as "the cook for an idealized version of the Old South."[37] While the character of Aunt Jemima had been a logo for the Aunt Jemima pancake brand (bought in 1926 by Quaker Oats, who sponsored the Disneyland restaurant), since the 1880s, this experience of her kitchen, billed as a "memorable visit to the Old South," was contextualized in Frontierland. The location (especially given that "the Old South" is generally not considered the American frontier) suggested that while black women may have existed in the formation of the American character, they were only a side note, subservient to the white experience.[38] The restaurant building itself was representative of "a fine Southern house, a lovely wooden building with pillars, elegant balconies with filigreed columns, and a porch area with a filigreed fence."[39] In contrast, Aunt Jemima wore "a red-and-white plaid dress, yellow tie and apron, and yellow-and-red kerchief on her head. She served tables, sang, and routinely took pictures with patrons."[40] While the name of the restaurant may suggest it "belongs" to Aunt Jemima, the contrast between the plantation style home and the servant-style garb worn by its namesake make it clear that she may be in charge of the kitchen, but she doesn't "live" in the house. Aunt Jemima's Pancake House later renamed Aunt Jemima's Kitchen, became a national chain. As the Civil Rights Movement swept the country, protests against the stereotyper became more vocal, and the character of Aunt Jemima ceased greeting guests when the restaurant was renamed Magnolia Tree Terrace in 1970 (a year before the rename of the Indian War Canoes). As with the Indian Village, the social movements of the 1960s and 1970s which called out Aunt Jemima and other caricatures across the nation as harmful stereotypes resulted in physical change on Disney landscapes.

The remaining vestiges of how glaringly white the 1950s national narrative was at Disney Parks are often more subtle than an entire othered "Indian Village," and are frequently most visible in their absence. After the removal of the Indian Village and Aunt Jemima's Pancake House no Disney Park attractions centered on the story of any people of color for many years, until the Disney Renaissance of the 1990s brought some non-white characters (Pocahontas, Aladdin, Mulan, etc.) into the Disney canon where they could provide inspiration for Disney Imagineers in their park updates. In the last ten years, Disney has endeavored more and more intensely to add layers of diversity to existing attractions where they can and have wholly recreated attractions to feature more diversity where they cannot. In addition to Alberta Falls, the "reimagined" Jungle Cruise characters include a Mexican artist, Rosa Soto Dominguez, a Japanese entomologist, Dr. Kon Chunosuke, and an Irish explorer, Siobhan Murphy. The Imagineers responsible for the retheming stated explicitly that they "set out to introduce a more inclusive perspective to the attraction."[41]

Another new layering of diversity is very much in evidence at the American Adventure pavilion at Epcot (part of Walt Disney World), where Disney devotes a small gallery to exhibits on American heritage that have included African, African

American and, most recently, American Indian art. The building that houses these exhibits also features the Mark Twain- and Benjamin Franklin-hosted theater show designed to take the viewer "through our nation's short, but storied history."[42] The content of the show, which premiered in 1982 (with updates in 1993 and 2007), represented what Mike Wallace called "an extraordinary step forward" in the American narrative at Disney in that "American history is no longer about great white men; indeed it seems to be largely about African Americans, women, Indians, and ecologists."[43] A Disney briefing pamphlet for employees at the pavilion confirmed that Disney "couldn't ignore certain major issues that questioned our nation's stand on human liberty and justice" when they designed the show.[44] While the show has made strides toward increasing the diversity of those featured, its white-centric roots nonetheless still resound—"our short but storied history" begins with European colonization, when the Pilgrims landed in the "New World" in 1620, with no mention of those already living in North America, and is still told from the perspective of two white men, Twain and Franklin.

In July 2018, Disney opened an exhibit of American Indian art in the "American Heritage Gallery," in the American Pavilion at Epcot. *Creating Tradition: Innovation and Change in American Indian Art*, a joint effort between Disney, the Smithsonian's National Museum of the American Indian (NMAI) and Museum of Indian Arts and Culture in Sante Fe, New Mexico (MIAC), is located directly outside the theater where Ben Franklin and Mark Twain narrate the greatest hits of American history ... beginning with the arrival of the pilgrims. The addition of *Creating Tradition* helps to complicate the narrative that already exists in the theatrical show, literally creating a layer of Native history on top of (or in this case, in front of) the show already in existence.[45] Through the juxtaposition of Native art from different time periods and geographic locations, *Creating* makes a simple but bold statement, given the location: American Indian peoples have always been here, they are still here, and they are not monolithic. At the exhibit's opening, NMAI Director Kevin Gover (Pawnee) captured both the intent of the exhibit and the importance of its location, stating that visitors would see that "the American Experience begins with the American Indians who have always been here ... This gallery helps to convey not only that there were a great many Indians and they were very different one from another, but also that they're still here."[46] Where the Indian Village portrayal of indigenous peoples ultimately made Native cultures a side note in a largely white story of colonization of the American frontier (no matter how faithfully Disney tried to recreate it), *Creating* starts from the Native perspective, centering their experience among other histories as opposed to sidelining them. By physically locating Native history within the American Adventure pavilion, Disney, NMAI and MIAC are furthering the growth of a more inclusive American narrative. Native cultures and American folk heroes not only occupy the same physical space but relate to one another not as adversaries (as in so many American folk histories of the "Old West," including Disney's own original Frontierland) but as part of one greater, unified story. The exhibit opening came in a year that saw increased American Indian representation in America writ large, with a record-breaking number of indigenous people running for office in the 2018 midterm elections, design selection for a National Native American Veterans Memorial to be built on the National Mall in Washington, D.C., and the critical success of *Coco* after its premiere in 2017.[47] As American Indian representation in the national narrative is further inscribed on the National Mall, it is also increasingly inscribed in the American Adventure at Walt Disney World.

In 2021 Disney opened another exhibition, *The Soul of Jazz: An American Adventure* in the American Adventure. Disney partnered with the New Orleans Jazz Museum, the American Jazz Museum in Kansas City, Missouri, and the National Jazz Museum in Harlem, New York, to bring together artwork from the Disney film *Soul*, which strongly featured jazz music and material culture artifacts such as Louis Armstrong's trumpet.[48] Situated across a rotunda from *Creating Tradition* and outside of the theater, the celebration of the "distinctly American art form" of jazz music that "originated by African Americans" and fused "the influences of many different cultures," according to the Disney press release about the show, is yet another layer of inclusive history recently laid on Disney's telling of the national narrative.[49]

FIGURE 6.1 Banners for *The Soul of Jazz* contrasted with the traditional narratives symbolized by the American Adventure pavilion and interactive of Emanuel Leutze's *Washington Crossing the Delaware* in 2022

Source: Courtesy of Christine Harrison for TouringPlans.com.

While some of Disney's attractions can be updated with layers, some must be wholly reimagined. Splash Mountain, a flume ride present on both coasts, was originally based on the 1946 Disney film "Song of the South," itself based on Joel Chandler Harris' Uncle Remus tales, both of which were criticized for inaccurate and racist depictions of African Americans in the post-Civil War south. Online petitions and calls to change the ride, which had occurred sporadically since its debut in 1989 at Disneyland and 1992 in Walt Disney World, increased in number in the late 2010s as America as a whole reckoned with the pandemic of racism.[50] In 2020, Disney announced a complete overhaul of the ride's theme, replacing animal characters like Br'er Rabbit who spoke in a stereotypical "Old South" African American dialect with a story centering on Tiana, the company's first black princess. Public Relations Director Michael Ramirez tied the retheme to the climate of the moment, saying "the retheming of Splash Mountain is of particular importance today. The new concept is inclusive ... and it speaks to the diversity of the millions of people who visit our parks each year."[51]

Conclusion

At the time Disney announced each of the changes discussed in this chapter, there was some public pushback from fans who were unhappy with the change, certainly not unexpected when one of the main themes of the park is nostalgia. In fostering nostalgia for both an America that never was and for past visits and times in guests' own lives, Disney Parks open themselves to the reality that when they change, those who are heavily invested in the nostalgia of a specific park as it lives in their memory may object. As one Disney employee put it "you can't move a bench without touching someone's memory."[52] In the past, this pushback has often come through letters written to the company or letters to the editors of local papers. With the advent of the internet, what used to be said in letters now appears on Disney blogs or Disney-centric message boards and social media, mostly staying within the Disney fan community. However, in 2021 when Disney announced the addition of a key of inclusivity to its "Four Keys" approach to service and detailed coming changes at the theme parks inspired by that key, some of the pushback on the internet went viral, offering a perfect example of where Disney theme parks sit in the national narrative, and what changes there represent to American identity.

On April 13, 2021, Chairman of Disney Parks, Experiences and Products Josh D'Amaro posted to the Disney Parks Blog an announcement of the Inclusion Key detailing what it would mean for the Disney Parks. The Key, wrote D'Amaro, would guide the company in

> ... cultivating an environment where all people feel welcomed and appreciated for their unique life experiences, perspectives and culture. Where we celebrate allyship and support for each other. And where diverse views and ideas are sought after as critical contributions towards our collective success.

He noted that the key reflects previously announced theme park updates including

> reimagining our attractions to be more inclusive, like upcoming enhancements to Jungle Cruise and new adventures with Princess Tiana. We're celebrating the diverse and inspiring stories of our cast and fans with creator collaborations and exciting experiences, like 'The Soul of Jazz' exhibit at Walt Disney World Resort.[53]

Though many of the changes had been announced previously, the company acknowledged that the timing of their announcements, most of which had rolled out between 2019 and 2021, coincided purposefully with the many public ways the larger American society was grappling with systemic racism.[54] "We are very mindful of the events that are happening around the world that impact people," Carmen Smith, head of inclusion strategies for Disney Imagineering was quoted as saying when the reimagined Jungle Cruise debuted to the public. "'The murder of George Floyd-the world responded to that in unique ways … there was an international response. How can we [Disney] be part of the healing journey of America?"[55] Likely, it is because the murder of George Floyd had sparked anew conversations about racial and social justice that D'Amaro's announcement became a flashpoint for many Americans, both Disney fans and non, on social media.

For example, a column posted to the *Orlando Sentinel's* online commentary section, written by Las Vegas Disney fan Jonathan VanBoskerck, quickly went viral for publicly claiming that "wokeness" was "ruining" the Disney theme park experience. The column, posted ten days after D'Amaro's announcement, derided the company's changes as taking a "politically woke scalpel" to the Walt Disney World he and his family knew, loved, and patronized for many years.[56] While VanBoskerck's stated concern was the way in which Disney acknowledged, or, in his words, "scream[ed] to the whole world that a decision has been made for political reasons" he admitted that as "a Christian and a conservative Republican" he felt that the politics espoused by Disney did not match his own, thus illustrating the larger conflict that Disney's inclusion key came to represent: Disney theme parks, to VanBoskerck and many others, represent American values. Disney's changing meant American values were changing, and VanBoskerck objected. Closing his piece, VanBoskerck asked Disney to "please return to the values and vision of Walt," which earlier he'd identified as patriotism and pro-capitalism. The plea, however, was heard not by Disney, but by other Americans, not just Disney fans, whose responses immediately flooded social media.

VanBoskerck's claim that "each of the changed scenes" in his former favorite ride, Pirates of the Caribbean, now reminds him "of reality and the politics that forced the changes" was read by Twitter user @girafecolore as "going to disney world with ur dad and he wont let you go on the pirates ride because it doesnt disrespect women enough."[57] The twitter thread tied to the article received thousands of similar comments, with most tying VanBoskerck's comments not to Disney specifically, but to the political moment. The political discourse in the

United States in the late 2010s and 2020s often framed those advocating for changes (both at Disney and society-wide) in service of social justice as liberal (usually Democrats) and those against as conservative (usually Republicans).[58] "Wokeness is the insult that Republicans came up with to describe someone who is aware, informed, and empathetic about an injustice" wrote @BetaRayBob1.[59] "He [VanBoskerck] likes free markets when it suits him," said @L_canoero, suggesting that the changes, which VanBoskerck had also tied to the company's "desire to make a profit" were the result of the will of the market to whom Disney is selling its experiences. Simultaneously, @L_canoero was suggesting that there was a cognitive dissonance in VanBoserck's claim that he didn't appreciate Disney's seeming political commentary, as Republicans are known to favor free markets, which VanBoserck suggested was driving the changes.[60] The tone of most of the responding tweets suggested that the author was at best out of step with the current political moment, and at worst, an example of everything wrong with conservatives in America. Even current politicians weighed in, with Val Demings, then the Congressional representative for Florida's 10th district—where Disney World resides, tweeting "I am proud to represent a community that is welcoming, tolerant, and always evolving to offer the best possible experience," an explicitly political lens for viewing change at the Disney theme park.[61]

This example reveals not merely a conflict of old versus new, generational memories or even understandings of history. As the replies to VanBoserck's opinion made clear, concern over change at Walt Disney World was being read by the online community as concern over changes in America writ large. This is a hallmark of disputes over public memory. The dispute over ways history is represented at Disney is not focused on what is "true" about the past, but rather, to quote John Bodnar, the dispute is over "serious matters in the present such as the nature of power and the question of loyalty to both official and vernacular cultures."[62]

While the Walt Disney Company may not relish it being done in public, Americans' ongoing debates about the way their theme parks change provide some of the best evidence that they indeed function as important sites of public memory for Americans. Further, these debates indicate that the tensions over changes at the Disney theme parks stand in for larger concerns in American society in general. Close reading of both the changes themselves and public reaction to them can help researchers of public memory understand the social mood at the time of the dispute. While debates continued on social media regarding Disney's inclusion key and subsequent retheming of certain rides, it was clear that Disney, through its own research and evolution in values, had foreseen and accepted the need to adapt. The company's recent decisions to increase inclusivity are described by the *Washington Post* as "a reflection of the times and country's consciousness, but also a business strategy as Disney needs a broader, more diverse audience to grow ... 'They have looked at the future and they have looked at the numbers and it's not a knee-jerk reaction.'"[63]

The Disney theme parks have adapted, slowly and often quietly, along with changes in American narratives since their creation. The physical landscape of the Disney theme parks is a three-dimensional record of American social and political change in the ways it adapts its representation of the national narrative over time. Disney theme parks might not be driving the national narrative, but they have been inscribing it on their buildings for the last 60 years for both historians and the public to read.

Notes

1 Marty Sklar quoted in Jim Korkis, *The Unofficial Walt Disney World 1971 Companion* (Theme Park Press, 2019), 54.
2 Linda Small, "Grave Goods and Social Identity at the Vietnam War Memorial," *Studies in Popular Culture*, 16, no. 2 (April 1994): 73.
3 Aisha Harris, "*Moana* Makes it Official: Disney Has Entered a Progressive, Inclusive Third Golden Age," *Slate*, November 21, 2016, https://slate.com/culture/2016/11/with-moana-frozen-big-hero-6-and-zootopia-disney-has-entered-an-inclusive-third-golden-age.html and Lila MacLellan, "There's a Timely Management Lesson in Disney and Pixar's Success with 'Coco'," *Quartz*, December 13, 2017, https://www.yahoo.com/news/timely-management-lesson-disney-pixar-143821091.html.
4 Tom Bricker, "Moana's Journey of Water Attraction Info," *Disney Tourist Blog*, April 2021, https://www.disneytouristblog.com/moana-journey-water-opening-info/ and Brady MacDonald, "Disneyland: World's first Disney/Pixar animation crossover coming to 'Mickey's Philharmagic'," *The Orange County Register*, July 2, 2021, https://www.ocregister.com/2021/07/01/disneyland-mickeys-philharmagic-adds-coco-characters-and-music-to-4d-concert-film/.
5 Allen Adamson, "Disney Knows It's Not Just Magic That Keeps a Brand on Top," *Forbes*, October 15, 2014, https://www.forbes.com/sites/allenadamson/2014/10/15/disney-knows-its-not-just-magic-that-keeps-a-brand-on-top/?sh=7c58214f5b26.
6 Gabrielle Russon, "Walt Disney Once Banned Alcohol. Now Orlando Theme Parks Say, 'Drink up'," *Orlando Sentinel*, September 11, 2018. https://www.orlandosentinel.com/business/tourism/os-bz-s4-theme-park-history-alcohol-20180907-story.html
7 Gabrielle Russon and DeWayne Bevil, "Disney Bans Smoking, Limits Stroller Size in Theme Parks," *Orlando Sentinel*, March 28, 2019, https://www.orlandosentinel.com/business/os-bz-disney-world-smoking-ban-20190308-story.html.
8 Hugo Martin, "Disneyland Plans a PC Makeover for its Pirates of the Caribbean Attraction," *Los Angeles Times*, July 2, 2017, https://latimes.com/business/la-fi-pirates-makeover-20170702-story.html.
    On a visit in 2021, the skipper of my boat stuck her foot over the railing of the boat to "shoe" the hippos away.
9 Originally, the guns shot lead pellets; they were changed to infrared versions in the 1980s.
10 Robert Johnson, "Disney Defends Right to Bear Toy Guns," *Orlando Sentinel*, October 28, 2002, https://www.orlandosentinel.com/news/os-xpm-2002-10-28–0210280253-story.html.
11 "The Disney Look," *Disney Careers*, accessed May 31, 2019, https://parks.disneycareers.com/the-disney-look.
12 Rick Rojas, "Disney Changes Dress Code to Allow Employees to Grow Beards," *Los Angeles Times*, January 24, 2012. https://latimes.com/entertainment/la-xpm-2012-jan-24-la-me-disney-look-20120124-story.html.
13 Alessa Dufresne, "Full List of 'Disney Look' Hairstyles, Nails, and Tattoos," *Inside the Magic*, April 14, 2021, https://insidethemagic.net/2021/04/disney-look-update-ad1/.
14 "More Americans Have Tattoos Today than Seven Years Ago," *Ipsos*, August 29, 2019, https://www.ipsos.com/en-us/news-polls/more-americans-have-tattoos-today.
    "Acceptable" tattoos may contain no offensive language/symbols or nudity, must be smaller than a hand-size, and not be on the face or neck. Kate Gibson, "Disney Will Let

Its Workers Sport Tattoos and Gender-Neutral Hairstyles," *CBSnews.com*, April 13, 2021, https://www.cbsnews.com/news/disney-tattoos-hairstyles-gender/.

15 *The Negro Motorist Green-Book*, also known as "The Green Book," scrutinized Disneyland in its early years and included it as a safe travel destination for African American families in its 1962 edition. Nearby similar destinations such as Knott's Berry Farm, conversely, never made the book's listings.

16 "1960 Census of the Population: Supplementary Reports: Race of the Population of the United States, by States: 1960." *Census.gov*, September 7, 1961. https://www.census.gov/library/publications/1961/dec/pc-s1–10.html.

17 Robert D. Shaw, Jr., "A $300-Million Fantasy World: Disney's Monument in Florida," *Miami Herald*, August 8, 1971, 1.

18 Between 2011 and 2012, 70% of new national landmarks were focused on "the diversity of the American experience," according to the National Park Service that oversees them. See the analysis of national park diversity by Jessica Goad, Matt Lee-Ashley, and Farah Z. Ahmand, "Better Reflecting Our Country's Growing Diversity," *Center for American Progress*, February 19, 2014, https://www.americanprogress.org/issues/green/reports/2014/02/19/84191/better-reflecting-our-countrys-growing-diversity/.

19 In talking of Disney's use of racial and gender stereotypes in the parks it is important to note, as Eric Avila says, that "Walt Disney cannot take credit for inventing these racial stereotypes. Rather, park designers drew on a tradition of racial stereotyping in the national culture." While Disney may strive to reflect the best of American character, it also reflects some of the worst parts. This affirms, however, its connection to the American narrative, particularly in the way it changes over time. Avila quoted in Sabrina Mittermeyer, *A Cultural History of the Disneyland Theme Parks: Middle Class Kingdoms* (Chicago: Intellect Books, 2021), 27.

20 For a history of the idea of separate spheres, see Linda K. Kerber, "Separate Spheres, Female Worlds, Woman's Place: The Rhetoric of Women's History," *The Journal of American History* 75, no. 1 (June 1988): 9–39, JSTOR.

21 A summary of the waves of feminism can be found at Constancy Grady, "The waves of feminism, and why people keep fighting over them, explained," *Vox*, July 20, 2018, https://www.vox.com/2018/3/20/16955588/feminism-waves-explained-first-second-third-fourth.

22 "Disneyland Eliminates Gender Roles," *Orlando Sentinel*, July 14, 1995, https://www.orlandosentinel.com/news/os-xpm-1995-07-14–9507140112-story.html.

23 Marla Jo Fisher, "Gender-Based Rules See Last Ride at Disneyland," *Baltimore Sun*, July 14, 1995, https://www.baltimoresun.com/news/bs-xpm-1995-07-14–1995195101-story.html.

24 Chris Woodyard, "Disneyland Giving Up Its Gender Bias," *Baltimore Sun*, May 15, 1995, https://www.baltimoresun.com/news/bs-xpm-1995-05-15–1995135103-story.html.

25 None of the sources indicated where the men were sourcing their information from, nor did the sources quote any of the female or male cast members who may have been directly affected.

26 Francoise Coste, "Conservative Women and Feminism in the United States: Between Hatred and Appropriation," *Caliban* 27 (2010): 167–176, https://doi.org/10.4000/caliban.2111.

27 Woodyard, "Disneyland Giving."

28 Park Ride History, "History of & Changes to Pirates of the Caribbean: Disneyland," YouTube video, 13:13, August 13, 2018, https://www.youtube.com/watch?v=BECOwsXkx1o and Joshua Shaffer, *Discovering the Magic Kingdom: An Unofficial Disneyland Vacation Guide* (Author House, 2010), 143.

29 "Pirates of the Caribbean," *MousePlanet*, nd, https://www.mouseplanet.com/guide/809/Disneyland-Resort/Disneyland-Park/New-Orleans-Square/Pirates-of-the-Caribbean.

30 Lindsay Brookshier, "Pirates of the Caribbean: A 50 Year History of Reflecting Modern Culture," *Disney Dose*, July 8, 2018, https://disneydose.com/pirates-of-the-caribbean-history/.

31 Dusty Sage cited in Mary Jo Fisher, "Say Goodbye to the Pirates of the Caribbean Bride Auction at Disneyland," *OC Register*, March 13, 2018, https://www.ocregister.com/2018/03/13/say-goodbye-to-the-pirates-of-the-caribbean-bride-auction-at-disneyland.

32 While no explicit claim is made by Disney as to Redd's sexual orientation or gender identity, scholars have long suggested that piracy was an occupation that allowed for gender nonconforming women and/or lesbian or bisexual women of the ancient world to find a safe place to be themselves, or at least an escape from a world that didn't accept them. See Marcus Rediker, "When Women Pirates Sailed the Seas," *The Wilson Quarterly* 17, no. 4 (1993): 102–110, JSTOR.

33 An approachable overview to one 1950s American history textbook can be found at Nathan Bernier, "What a 1950s Texas Textbook Can Teach Us About Today's Textbook Fight," *KUT 90.5*, November 6, 2016, https://www.kut.org/education/2016-11-16/what-a-1950s-texas-textbook-can-teach-us-about-todays-textbook-fight. An in-depth history of American approaches to education can be found in Gerald L. Gutek, *An Historical Introduction to American Education* (Long Grove, Illinois: Waveland Press, Inc., 2012).

34 Ernest Lenn, "Paleface Disney's AGVA Hiawatha," *San Francisco Examiner*, August 18, 1957, 13.

35 While a longer academic discussion of how Disneyland's Indian Village, Indian War Canoes and other representations of indigenous life and history relate to the time in which they were created, to the historic record, and to today is certainly warranted, it does not fit within the scope of this project. Jim Korkis, "Disneyland's Indian Village," *MousePlanet*, April 28, 2021, https://www.mouseplanet.com/12930/Disneylands_Indian_Village. For an overview of Native representation over time at Walt Disney World, see Victoria Lantz, "What's Missing in Frontierland? American Indian Culture and Indexical Absence at Walt Disney World, in *Performance and the Disney Theme Park Experience*, ed. J. Kokai and T Robson (New York: Palgrave Macmillan, 2019), 43–63.

36 Anecdotal evidence attributes the demise of the Indian Village to "labor disputes" between the native actors and Disney (See Korkis, "Disneyland's Indian Village"). More study is needed to determine whether these disputes were in fact directly tied to increased focus on the part of the actors on self-determination of their space in the national narrative write large. For more on Alcatraz's occupation as an impetus for the Red Power movement see Carolyn Strange and Tina Loo, "Holding the Rock: The'Indianization' of Alcatraz Island, 1969–1999," *The Public Historian* 23, no. 1 (Winter 2001), 55–74.

37 The Jemima character derived from early minstrel shows; the character was wholly created to humor white audiences. See Maurice Manring, "Aunt Jemima Explained: The Old South, the Absent Mistress, and the Slave in a Box," *Southern Cultures* 2, no. 1 (Fall 1995), 19–44.

38 "Famed Aunt Jemima Will Cook," *Independent Press Telegram* [Long Beach, CA], July 15, 1955, 8.

39 Fran Rosen and Franklin Hughes, "Aunt Jemima's Kitchen," *Ferris State University Jim Crow Museum*, 2019, https://www.ferris.edu/HTMLS/news/jimcrow/question/2019/april_may.htm.

40 Rosen and Hughes.

41 Brooke Geiger McDonald, "Exclusive: Disney Imagineers talk new Jungle Cruise characters, S.E.A. connections, and Trader Sam's," *Attractions Magazine*, March 19, 2021, https://attractionsmagazine.com/exclusive-disney-imagineers-talk-new-jungle-cruise-characters-s-e-a-connections-and-trader-sams/.

42 "The American Adventure," *Walt Disney World*, accessed May 17, 2018. https://disneyworld.disney.go.com/attractions/epcot/american-adventure/.

43 Mike Wallace, *Mickey Mouse History and Other Essays on American Memory* (Philadelphia: Temple University Press, 1996), 151.

44 Quoted in Wallace, 151.

45 The gallery's originator, Van Romans, explained that the intent behind the gallery was to offer space for Disney to tell a fuller story of America. "Hopefully it's a story about our own

diversity and our own sense of who we are as a country," Romans said. Bethanee Bemis, "Epcot Just Got a New Smithsonian Museum Exhibition," *Smithsonian Magazine*, August 22, 2018, https://www.smithsonianmag.com/smithsonian-institution/epcot-just-got-new-smithsonian-museum-exhibition-180969985/.

46 Kevin Gover, Creating Tradition Opening (notes taken during speech, attended in person in Orlando, Florida, July 27, 2018).

47 Leila Fadel, "Record Number of Native Americans Running for Office in Midterms," *National Public Radio*, July 4, 2018, https://www.npr.org/2018/07/04/625425037/record-number-of-native-americans-running-for-office-in-midterms.

48 The show is also set to tour in New Orleans, Kansas City and New York.

49 "EPCOT Unveils 'The Soul of Jazz: An American Adventure' Exhibition in American Adventure Pavilion," *Walt Disney World News*, February 1, 2021, https://wdwnews.com/releases/epcot-unveils-the-soul-of-jazz-an-american-adventure-exhibit-at-the-american-adventure-pavilion/.

50 Austin Horn, "Disney Announces Redesign of Splash Mountain After Some Call Ride Theme Racist," *National Public Radio*, June 25, 2020, https://www.npr.org/sections/live-updates-protests-for-racial-justice/2020/06/25/883507841/disney-announces-redesign-of-splash-mountain-after-some-call-ride-themes-racist, Carly Mallenbaum, "Why people are petitioning Disney to give Splash Mountain a 'Princess and the Frog' Makeover," *USA Today*, June 11, 2020, https://www.usatoday.com/story/travel/news/2020/06/11/splash-mountain-disney-petition-princess-frog/5347879002/.

51 Michael Ramirez, "New Adventures with Princess Tiana Coming to Disneyland Park and Magic Kingdom Park," *Disney Parks Blog*, June 25, 2020, https://disneyparks.disney.go.com/blog/2020/06/new-adventures-with-princess-tiana-coming-to-disneyland-park-and-magic-kingdom-park/.

52 Todd Martens, "A Course Correction," *Los Angeles Times*, July 19, 2021, E1.

53 Josh D'Amaro, "A Place Where Everyone Is Welcome," *Disney Parks Blog*, April 13, 2021, https://disneyparks.disney.go.com/blog/2021/04/a-place-where-everyone-is-welcome/.

54 See, for example, Justin Worland, "America's Long Overdue Awakening to Systemic Racism," *Time*, June 11, 2020, https://time.com/5851855/systemic-racism-america/.

55 Martens, "A course." Smith specifically referred to the murder of George Floyd, a black man murdered by a white police officer in Minneapolis on May 25, 2020. His murder sparked racial justice protests across the United States.

56 Jonathan VanBoskerck, "I Love Visiting Disney World but Wokeness Is Ruining the Experience," *Orlando Sentinel*, April 25, 2021, A14.

57 @girafecolore, Twitter post, April 23, 2021, 11:31 am, https://twitter.com/girafecolore/status/1385617437333282816?ref_src=twsrc%5Etfw%7Ctwcamp%5Etweetembed%7Ctwterm%5E1385617437333282816%7Ctwgr%5E%7Ctwcon%5Es1_&ref_url=https%3A%2F%2Fwww.scarymommy.com%2Fdisney-woke-op-ed%2F.

58 See Orlando Sentinel, Twitter post, April 23, 2021, 9:08 am, https://twitter.com/orlandosentinel/status/1385581448363716608.

59 @BetaRayBob1, Twitter post, April 23, 2012, 12:53 pm, https://twitter.com/BetaRayBob1/status/1385637951246413827.

60 @L_canero, Twitter post, April 24, 2021, 1:03 pm, https://twitter.com/L_canoero/status/1386002944777142276.

61 @RepValDemings, Twitter post, April 23, 2021, 11:53 am, https://twitter.com/RepValDemings/status/1385622797716688900.

62 John Bodnar, "Public Memory in an American City: Commemoration in Cleveland," in *Commemorations: The Politics of National Identity*," edited by John R. Gillis (Princeton: Princeton University Press, 1994), 76.

63 Hannah Sampson, "Anti-racism, Tattoos and No More 'Wench Auctions:' Disney's 'Woke' Moves Spark a Conservative Backlash," *Washington Post*, May 7, 2021.

References

"1960 Census of the Population: Supplementary Reports: Race of the Population of the United States, by States: 1960." *Census.gov*, September 7, 1961. https://www.census.gov/library/publications/1961/dec/pc-s1–10.html

@BetaRayBob1. Twitter post, April 23, 2012, 12:53 pm. https://twitter.com/BetaRayBob1/status/1385637951246413827

@girafecolore. Twitter post, April 23, 2021, 11:31 am. https://twitter.com/girafecolore/status/1385617437333282816?ref_src=twsrc%5Etfw%7Ctwcamp%5Etweetembed%7Ctwterm%5E1385617437333282816%7Ctwgr%5E%7Ctwcon%5Es1_&ref_url=https%3A%2F%2Fwww.scarymommy.com%2Fdisney-woke-op-ed%2F

@L_canero. Twitter post, April 24, 2021, 1:03 pm. https://twitter.com/L_canoero/status/1386002944777142276

@OrlandoSentinel. Twitter post, April 23, 2021, 9:08 am. https://twitter.com/orlandosentinel/status/1385581448363716608

@RepValDemings. Twitter post, April 23, 2021, 11:53 am. https://twitter.com/RepValDemings/status/1385622797716688900

Adamson, Allen. "Disney Knows It's Not Just Magic That Keeps a Brand on Top." *Forbes*, October 15, 2014. https://www.forbes.com/sites/allenadamson/2014/10/15/disney-knows-its-not-just-magic-that-keeps-a-brand-on-top/?sh=7c58214f5b26

Bemis, Bethanee. "Epcot Just Got a New Smithsonian Museum Exhibition." *Smithsonian Magazine*, August 22, 2018. https://www.smithsonianmag.com/smithsonian-institution/epcot-just-got-new-smithsonian-museum-exhibition-180969985/

Bernier, Nathan. "What a 1950s Texas Textbook Can Teach Us About Today's Textbook Fight." *KUT 90.5*, November 6, 2016. https://www.kut.org/education/2016-11-16/what-a-1950s-texas-textbook-can-teach-us-about-todays-textbook-fight

Bricker, Tom. "Moana's Journey of Water Attraction Info." *Disney Tourist Blog*, April 2021. https://www.disneytouristblog.com/moana-journey-water-opening-info/

Bodnar, John, "Public Memory in an American City: Commemoration in Cleveland." In *Commemorations: The Politics of National Identity*, edited by John R. Gillis, 74–89. Princeton: Princeton University Press, 1994.

Brookshier, Lindsay. "Pirates of the Caribbean: A 50 Year History of Reflecting Modern Culture." *Disney Dose*, July 8, 2018. https://disneydose.com/pirates-of-the-caribbean-history/

Coste, Francoise. "Conservative Women and Feminism in the United States: Between Hatred and Appropriation." *Caliban*, Vol. 27 (2010): 167–176. 10.4000/caliban.2111.

D'Amaro, Josh. "A Place Where Everyone is Welcome." *Disney Parks Blog*, April 13, 2021. https://disneyparks.disney.go.com/blog/2021/04/a-place-where-everyone-is-welcome/

"Disneyland Eliminates Gender Roles." *Orlando Sentinel*, July 14, 1995. https://www.orlandosentinel.com/news/os-xpm-1995-07-14–9507140112-story.html

Dufresne, Alessa. "Full List of 'Disney Look' Hairstyles, Nails, and Tattoos." *Inside the Magic*, April 14, 2021. https://insidethemagic.net/2021/04/disney-look-update-ad1/

"EPCOT Unveils 'the Soul of Jazz: An American Adventure' Exhibition in American Adventure Pavilion." *Walt Disney World News*, February 1, 2021. https://wdwnews.com/releases/epcot-unveils-the-soul-of-jazz-an-american-adventure-exhibit-at-the-american-adventure-pavilion/

Fadel, Leila. "Record Number of Native Americans Running for Office in Midterms." *National Public Radio*, July 4, 2018. https://www.npr.org/2018/07/04/625425037/record-number-of-native-americans-running-for-office-in-midterms

"Famed Aunt Jemima Will Cook." *Independent Press Telegram* [Long Beach, CA], July 15, 1955.

Fisher, Marla Jo. "Gender-Based Rules See Last Ride at Disneyland." *Baltimore Sun*, July 14, 1995. https://www.baltimoresun.com/news/bs-xpm-1995-07-14–1995195101-story.html

Fisher, Mary Jo. "Say Goodbye to the Pirates of the Caribbean Bride Auction at Disneyland." *OC Register*, March 13, 2018. https://www.ocregister.com/2018/03/13/say-goodbye-to-the-pirates-of-the-caribbean-bride-auction-at-disneyland

Gibson, Kate. "Disney Will Let Its Workers Sport Tattoos and Gender-Neutral Hairstyles." *CBSnews.com*, April 13, 2021. https://www.cbsnews.com/news/disney-tattoos-hairstyles-gender/

Goad, Jessica, Matt Lee-Ashley and Farah Z. Ahmand. "Better Reflecting Our Country's Growing Diversity." *Center for American Progress*, February 19, 2014. https://www.americanprogress.org/issues/green/reports/2014/02/19/84191/better-reflecting-our-countrys-growing-diversity/

Grady, Constance. "The Waves of Feminism, and Why People Keep Fighting Over Them, Explained." *Vox*, July 20, 2018. https://www.vox.com/2018/3/20/16955588/feminism-waves-explained-first-second-third-fourth

Gutek, Gerald L. *An Historical Introduction to American Education*. Long Grove, Illinois: Waveland Press, Inc., 2012.

Harris, Aisha. "*Moana* Makes it Official: Disney Has Entered a Progressive, Inclusive Third Golden Age." *Slate*, November 21, 2016. https://slate.com/culture/2016/11/with-moana-frozen-big-hero-6-and-zootopia-disney-has-entered-an-inclusive-third-golden-age.html

Horn, Austin. "Disney Announces Redesign of Splash Mountain After Some Call Ride Theme Racist." *National Public Radio*, June 25, 2020. https://www.npr.org/sections/live-updates-protests-for-racial-justice/2020/06/25/883507841/disney-announces-redesign-of-splash-mountain-after-some-call-ride-themes-racist

Johnson, Robert. "Disney Defends Right to Bear Toy Guns." *Orlando Sentinel*, October 28, 2002. https://www.orlandosentinel.com/news/os-xpm-2002-10-28–0210280253-story.html

Kerber, Linda K. "Separate Spheres, Female Worlds, Woman's Place: The Rhetoric of Women's History." *The Journal of American History*, Vol. 75, no. 1 (June 1988): 9–39.

Korkis, Jim. "Disneyland's Indian Village." *MousePlanet*, April 28, 2021. https://www.mouseplanet.com/12930/Disneylands_Indian_Village

Korkis, Jim. *The Unofficial Walt Disney World 1971 Companion*. Theme Park Press, 2019.

Lantz, Victoria. "What's Missing in Frontierland? American Indian Culture and Indexical Absence at Walt Disney World." In *Performance and the Disney Theme Park Experience*, edited by J. Kokai and T. Robson, 43–63. New York: Palgrave Macmillan, 2019.

Lenn, Ernest. "Paleface Disney's AGVA Hiawatha." *San Francisco Examiner*, August 18, 1957.

MacDonald, Brady. "Disneyland: World's First Disney/Pixar Animation Crossover Coming to Mickey's Philharmagic" *The Orange County Register*, July 2, 2021. https://www.ocregister.com/2021/07/01/disneyland-mickeys-philharmagic-adds-coco-characters-and-music-to-4d-concert-film/

MacLellan, Lila. "There's a Timely Management Lesson in Disney and Pixar's Success with 'Coco'." *Quartz*, December 13, 2017. https://www.yahoo.com/news/timely-management-lesson-disney-pixar-143821091.html

Mallenbaum, Carly. "Why People Are Petitioning Disney to Give Splash Mountain a 'Princess and the Frog' Makeover." *USA Today*, June 11, 2020. https://www.usatoday.com/story/travel/news/2020/06/11/splash-mountain-disney-petition-princess-frog/5347879002/

Manring, Maurice. "Aunt Jemima Explained: The Old South, the Absent Mistress, and the Slave in a Box." *Southern Cultures*, Vol. 2, no. 1 (Fall 1995), 19–44.

Martens, Todd. "A course correction." *Los Angeles Times*, July 19, 2021.

Martin, Hugo. "Disneyland Plans a PC Makeover for Its Pirates of the Caribbean Attraction." *Los Angeles Times*, July 2, 2017. https://latimes.com/business/la-fi-pirates-makeover-20170702-story.html

McDonald, Brooke Geiger. "Exclusive: Disney Imagineers Talk New Jungle Cruise Characters, S.E.A. Connections, and Trader Sam's." *Attractions Magazine*, March 19, 2021. https://attractionsmagazine.com/exclusive-disney-imagineers-talk-new-jungle-cruise-characters-s-e-a-connections-and-trader-sams/

Mittermeyer, Sabrina. *A Cultural History of the Disneyland Theme Parks: Middle Class Kingdoms*. Chicago: Intellect Books, 2021.

"More Americans Have Tattoos Today than Seven Years Ago." *Ipsos*, August 29, 2019. https://www.ipsos.com/en-us/news-polls/more-americans-have-tattoos-today

Park Ride History. "History of & Changes to Pirates of the Caribbean: Disneyland." YouTube video, 13:13, August 13, 2018. https://www.youtube.com/watch?v=BEC0wsXkx1o

"Pirates of the Caribbean." *MousePlanet*, n.d. https://www.mouseplanet.com/guide/809/Disneyland-Resort/Disneyland-Park/New-Orleans-Square/Pirates-of-the-Caribbean

Ramirez, Michael. "New Adventures with Princess Tiana Coming to Disneyland Park and Magic Kingdom Park." *Disney Parks Blog*, June 25, 2020. https://disneyparks.disney.go.com/blog/2020/06/new-adventures-with-princess-tiana-coming-to-disneyland-park-and-magic-kingdom-park/

Rediker, Marcus. "When Women Pirates Sailed the Seas." *The Wilson Quarterly*, Vol. 17, no. 4 (1993): 102–110.

Rojas, Rick. "Disney Changes Dress Code to Allow Employees to Grow Beards." *Los Angeles Times*, January 24, 2012. https://latimes.com/entertainment/la-xpm-2012-jan-24-la-me-disney-look-20120124-story.html

Rosen, Fran and Franklin Hughes. "Aunt Jemima's Kitchen." *Ferris State University Jim Crow Museum*. 2019. https://www.ferris.edu/HTMLS/news/jimcrow/question/2019/april_may.htm

Russon, Gabrielle. "Walt Disney Once Banned Alcohol. Now Orlando Theme Parks Say, 'Drink up." *Orlando Sentinel*, September 11, 2018. https://www.orlandosentinel.com/business/tourism/os-bz-s4-theme-park-history-alcohol-20180907-story.html

Russon, Gabrielle and DeWayne Bevil. "Disney Bans Smoking, Limits Stroller Size in Theme Parks." *Orlando Sentinel*, March 28, 2019. https://www.orlandosentinel.com/business/os-bz-disney-world-smoking-ban-20190308-story.html

Sampson, Hannah. "Anti-racism, Tattoos and No More 'Wench Auctions:' Disney's 'Woke' Moves Spark a Conservative Backlash." *Washington Post*, May 7, 2021.

Shaffer, Joshua. *Discovering the Magic Kingdom: An Unofficial Disneyland Vacation Guide*. Author House, 2010.

Shaw, Jr., and D. Robert. "A $300-Million Fantasy World: Disney's Monument in Florida." *Miami Herald*, August 8, 1971.

Small, Linda. "Grave Goods and Social Identity at the Vietnam War Memorial." *Studies in Popular Culture*, Vol. 16, no. 2 (April 1994): 73–84.

Strange, Carolyn and Tina Loo. "Holding the Rock: The 'Indianization' of Alcatraz Island, 1969-1999." *The Public Historian*, Vol. 23, no. 1 (Winter 2001): 55–74.

"The American Adventure." *Walt Disney World*. Accessed May 17, 2018. https://disneyworld.disney.go.com/attractions/epcot/american-adventure/

"The Disney Look." *Disney Career*. Accessed May 31, 2019. https://parks.disneycareers.com/the-disney-look

VanBoskerck, Jonathan. "I Love Visiting Disney World but Wokeness Is Ruining the Experience." *Orlando Sentinel*, April 25, 2021.

Woodyard, Chris. "Disneyland Giving Up Its Gender Bias." *Baltimore Sun*, May 15, 1995. https://www.baltimoresun.com/news/bs-xpm-1995-05-15–1995135103-story.html

Worland, Justin. "America's Long Overdue Awakening to Systemic Racism." *Time*, June 11, 2020. https://time.com/5851855/systemic-racism-america/

CONCLUSION: A NEW UNDERSTANDING OF "DISNEYFICATION"

In 2022 the Smithsonian's National Museum of American History put out a call to the public "for images that capture *your* experiences as guests at Disneyland and Walt Disney World."[1] Within two weeks, over 6,000 people had responded with over 30,000 images, eager to share their memories. The stories and images shared ranged from heartwarming to heartbreaking, dated July 1955 to February 2022, and came from both lifelong fans and one-time visitors. While their details were different, all the stories shared highlighted how deeply entrenched and meaningful the memories of their Disney Park visit were to the submitters. Many emphasized themes such as the making of intergenerational and collective memories, the role of the entire Disney Park experience in creating those memories, and the ties between a visit to a Disney Park and understanding "American" identity.[2]

It is difficult to overstate the importance of the Disney brand in American culture and identity-making. The Disney theme parks are on par with and even rival some federal sites of memory in their effectiveness as locations of dissemination and negotiation of a national narrative. Yet the ways in which that narrative is represented at Disney theme parks are not, of course, immune to criticism. As this book has shown, both the public and the academy continue to reproach the company for being slow to reflect larger cultural changes. It is important to understand where Disney is taking their content cues from. While they are sometimes informed by the work of academics, the updates Disney has executed in galleries and attractions reflect the changes pushed for by the public at large, both on Disney property and in the country as a whole. Disney has received criticism for its presentation of history, but they have not ignored it. Rather, the changes made at their parks reflect those desired perhaps not by all of their critics, but by their ultimate stakeholders, the ticket-purchasing public, which are not always one and the same with the changes suggested by academics or even social activists.

DOI: 10.4324/9781003315094-10

This is not to absolve Disney from examination or discount potentially problematic aspects to their presentation of history. Rather, it is to suggest that in order to make the best use of the sometimes-fraught relationship that Disney has with public history and the national story, consumers should seek ways in which to examine Disney constructively, beyond merely denunciation or deification. Steven Watts noted that the polarizing strife between "Disney Disciples" and "Disney Denouncers" has "created an emotional and ideological minefield for those who wish to approach Disney seeking neither revelation nor damnation, but understanding."[3] While many historians and cultural critics acknowledge Disney's importance, they have lamented it, or worse, spent their energy criticizing its consumers, those, like the very people who submitted to the National Museum of American History's Disney stories project, who find comfort, identity, or even just entertainment in Disney's products. When Disney announced its purchase of the American Broadcasting Company in 1995, a professor of humanities at Yale declared "At the end of this road lies cultural homogenization of the most ghastly kind … It's a disaster." Other academics quoted at the time suggested that "the taste of the Disney products has always seemed to be gravely sub-adult" and "what's happening is that we're all being dragged down to this infantile level."[4] These types of analyses and statements are alienating to a public that very clearly enjoy Disney's product and leave no room for asking questions that illuminate what the public is taking from those products. These dismissive statements also limit opportunities for developing ways to use Disney's popularity to engage the public and The Walt Disney Company constructively in discussions of history and national identity.

To that end, a new understanding of the terms "Mickey Mouse history" and "Disneyfication" are in order. Those terms have often been used to denote superficiality and commercialism in Disney's use of history, a way for users to dismiss Disney's history as unworthy of discussion or engagement. The terms have even come to be used beyond Disney products. In 2022, Merriam-Webster defines "Mickey Mouse" as "too easy, small, ineffective, or unimportant to be taken seriously" and "Disneyfication" as "the transformation (as of something real or unsettling) into carefully controlled and safe entertainment or an environment with similar qualities."[5] What is occurring at the Disney Parks when history is "Disneyfied" is not just the creating of a "safe" version of history, though that is a valid charge. It is the public and the Disney corporation engaging to craft a version of American history that reflects who the American people want to be. That certainly isn't too "unimportant to be taken seriously," as is implied when it is charged with being "Mickey Mouse history." Rather, it is the very heart of how the public uses history to find meaning in their daily lives, and worthy of not only academic interest but our respect as well. Both the official definition of Disneyfication and the one suggested here acknowledge that the "history" presented isn't factually true to the events, but one version dismisses the role of the public in the exchange, negating their agency and casting them merely as consumers. If we can reframe our thinking, we might instead understand and define "Disneyfication" as a location-specific process by which the public and a corporation are engaged in a cultural ritual of transforming historical fact into the "national narrative."

By reinjecting the agency of the public into our understanding of what is happening at the Disney Parks, we might begin to better see the ways in which the public use the Disney Parks as places to influence the national narrative. From their calls for shifting the way women are represented in certain attractions, a park-specific demand, to calls made on Disney property to change the country's DACA laws, a nationwide influence, the public has always used Disney as a platform for shaping American identities. Because Disney Park visitors are a self-selecting group, it cannot be said that they represent an impartial cross-section of the American public. However, their views as they influence the Disney theme parks may still offer a useful tool to assess how Americans relate to history. If we understand how the public uses history at Disney, we will be better positioned to work with both Disney and the public to facilitate that use in responsible ways.

Further, this approach can and should be applied to other sites of public memory that occupy a somewhat "gray" space in the national narrative; places such as The Henry Ford, Colonial Williamsburg, Six Flags America and Knott's Berry Farm that are nonfederal sites yet tell stories of American history and identity. Foregrounding public agency at these locations allows public historians to build a more constructive analysis of sites of public memory and the way the public uses them, rather than falling into the all-too-easy answer of dismissing entertaining versions of American stories as "unreal" or "Mickey Mouse," and thus unworthy of either study or professional engagement.

Walt Disney was not the first to use history to inspire his storytelling nor the first to turn history into a physical experience. He was, however, the first to use a brand that had itself already become symbolic of a nation's history to create that physical experience. Over time, the Disney theme parks have been elevated to nationally important places of collective memory of the American experience. The factors in this rise help us to understand why, if Disney wasn't the first to do many of these things, they nevertheless became perhaps the most important to have done so.

The castles, the Magic Kingdom, EPCOT, Frontierland, they all reflect those of us in the United States, our national narrative, and we in turn participate in reshaping Disney's narrative into our own constantly morphing image. Understanding how Disney theme parks came to play such an important function can also provide a key to understanding how the national narrative is shaped in other locations of collective memory as well. The factors of influence outlined here provide an initial framework for future researchers to explore how other non-federal locations of memory gain cultural influence, how the public works with or against private corporations to shape the story of the nation they reflect. The story of Disney's ascendence as a site of national identity-making also offers us a way to constructively use Disney Parks to further our understanding of the state of the national narrative if we are willing to understand its role as a physical place for identity negotiation. This shift in understanding might even help public historians to untangle the complicated question of exactly how "Disney" came to mean so much to so many.

Notes

1 "Disney Parks and American Stories," *National Museum of American History*, https://americanhistory.si.edu/disney-parks-and-american-stories.
2 The submissions also pointed to areas that warrant future study, including an expansion of the analysis to Disneyland's California Adventure, Disney's Hollywood Studios, Disney's Animal Kingdom, and the rest of Epcot. Other future avenues of inquiry include the influence of Disney's North American theme parks on international visitors' understanding of America and the effect of the international Disney Park's representations of America abroad on visitors of all nationalities.
3 Steven Watts, "Walt Disney: Art and Politics in the American Century," *The Journal of American History* 82, no. 1 (June 1995): 84.
   Jason Sperb has offered an excellent short analysis of the problems of teaching Disney when most students come to his classroom firmly rooted in one camp or another. Sperb suggests that the goal for those teaching the subject of Disney should be to "inform, but not necessarily change, minds and to get students to be reflective, not critical." Jason Sperb, "How (Not) to Teach Disney," *Journal of Film and Video* 70, no. 1 (Spring 2018): 47–60. This is a perfect description of how public historians should approach the subject as well, simply replacing "students" with "the public."
4 Harold Bloom, Paul Fussell and Len Sweet quoted in Mitchell Landsberg, "Disney's World Inescapable," *Albuquerque Journal*, August 6, 1995, 48.
5 *Merriam-Webster s.v.* "Mickey Mouse," accessed April 12, 2022, https://www.merriam-webster.com/dictionary/Mickey%20Mouse and *Merriam-Webster s.v.* "Disneyfication," accessed April 12, 2022, https://www.merriam-webster.com/dictionary/Disneyfication.

References

Francaviglia, Richard. "History After Disney: The Significance of 'Imagineered' Historical Places," *The Public Historian*, Vol. 17, no. 4 (Autumn 1995): 69–74.

Landsberg, Mitchell. "Disney's World Inescapable." *Albuquerque Journal*, August 6, 1995.

Merriam-Webster s.v. "Disneyfication." Accessed April 12, 2022. https://www.merriam-webster.com/dictionary/Disneyfication.

Merriam-Webster s.v. "Mickey Mouse." Accessed April 12, 2022. https://www.merriam-webster.com/dictionary/Mickey%20Mouse.

Sperb, Jason. "How (Not) to Teach Disney." *Journal of Film and Video*, Vol. 70, no. 1 (Spring 2018): 47–60.

Watts, Steven. "Walt Disney: Art and Politics in the American Century." *The Journal of American History*, Vol. 82, no. 1 (June 1995): 84–110.

INDEX